CLASSIC ROCK
50 FAVORITES
for Easy Guitar

Project Manager: Aaron Stang
Book Art Layout: Ken Rehm

CONTENTS

ARTIST INDEX

ALL I WANNA DO

Words and Music by
SHERYL CROW, WYN COOPER,
BILL BOTTRELL, DAVID BAERWALD
and KEVIN GILBERT

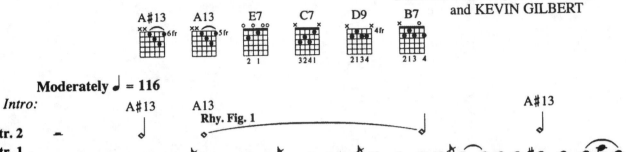

All I Wanna Do - 6 - 1

10

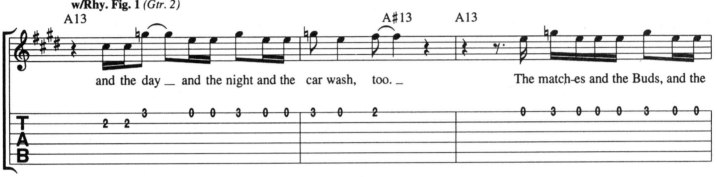

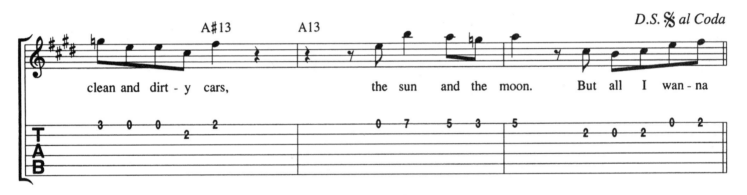

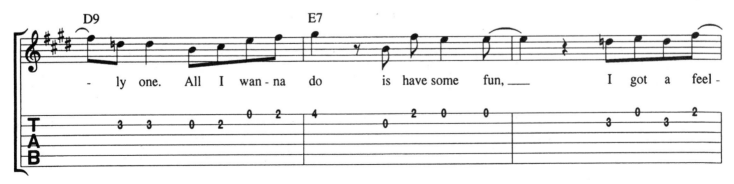

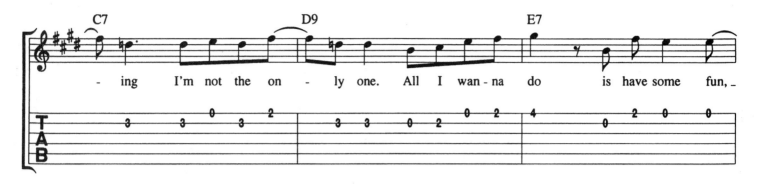

Verse 2:
I like a good beer buzz early in the morning,
And Billy likes to peel the labels from his bottles of Bud
And shreds them on the bar.
Then he lights every match in an oversized pack,
Letting each one burn down to his thick fingers
Before blowing and cursing them out.
And he's watching the Buds as they spin on the floor.
A happy couple enters the bar dancing dangerously close to one another.
The bartender looks up from his wants ads.
(To Chorus:)

BAD MOON RISING

Words and Music by
JOHN C. FOGERTY

Bad Moon Rising - 5 - 2

BORN TO RUN

Words and Music by
BRUCE SPRINGSTEEN

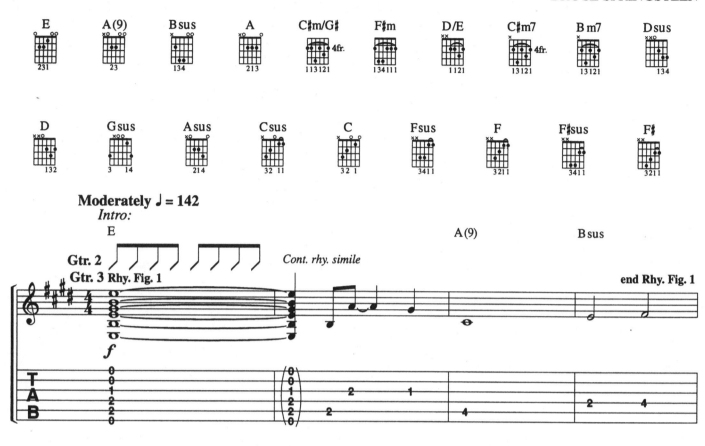

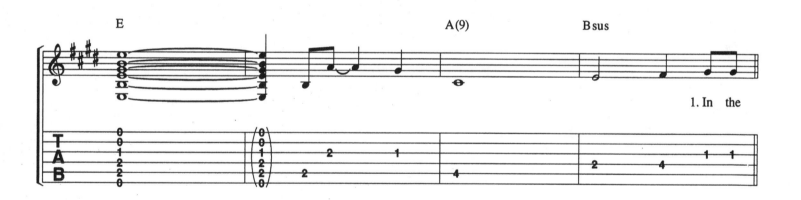

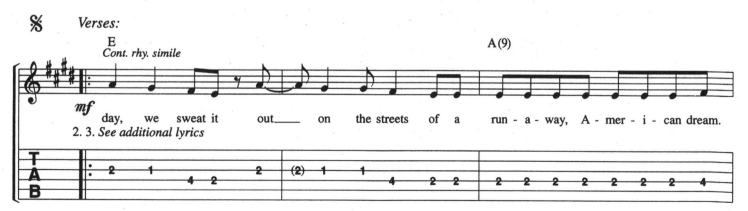

18

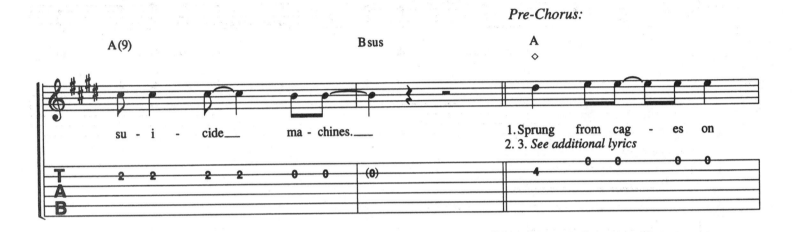

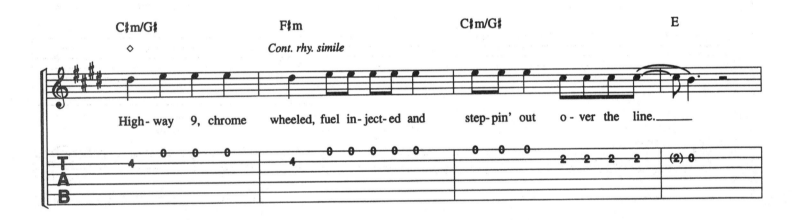

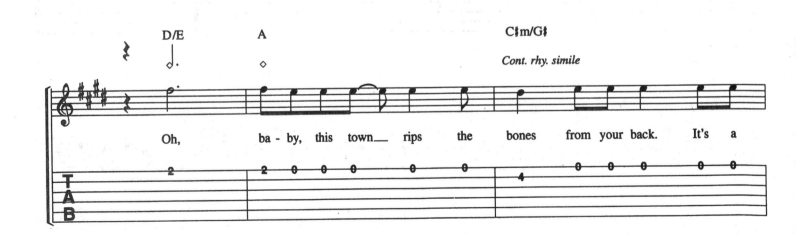

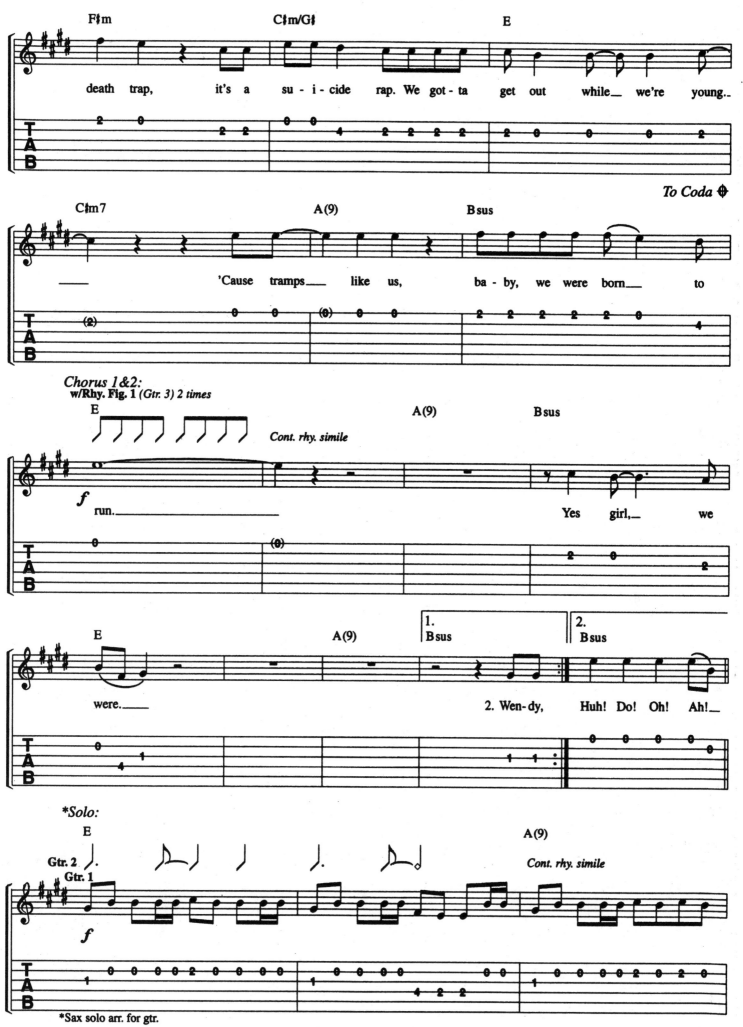

Born to Run - 7 - 3

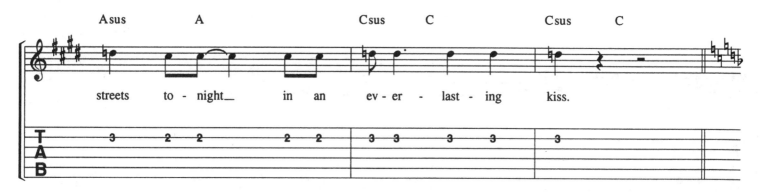

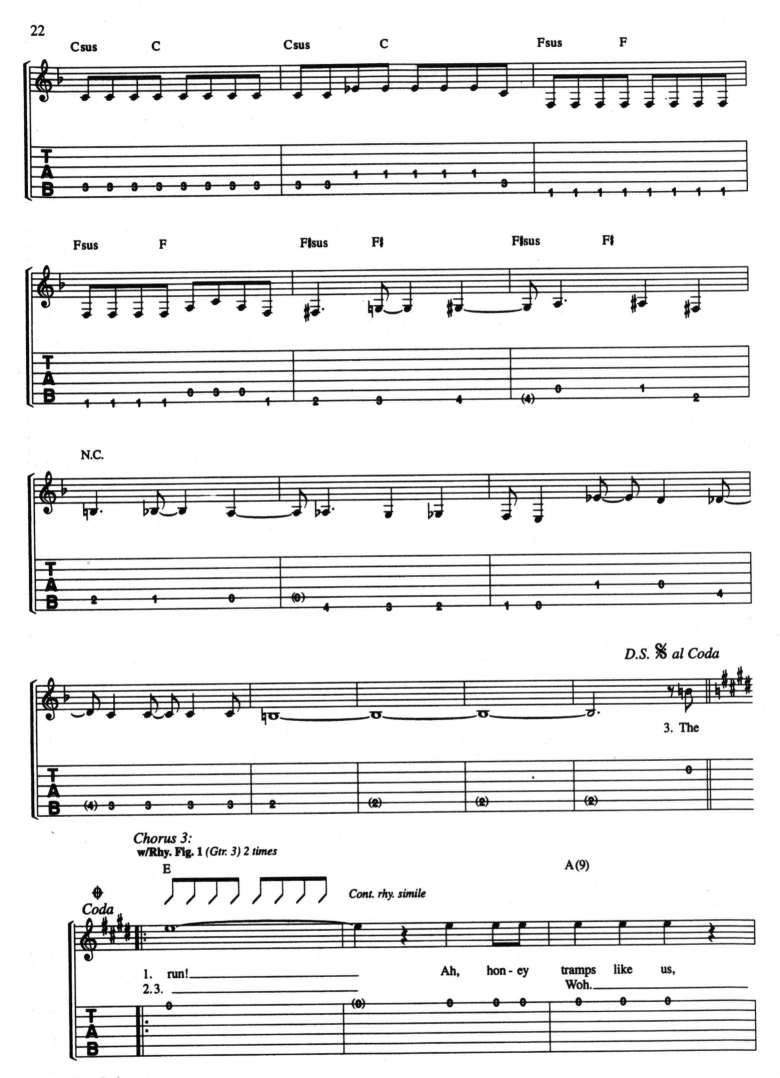

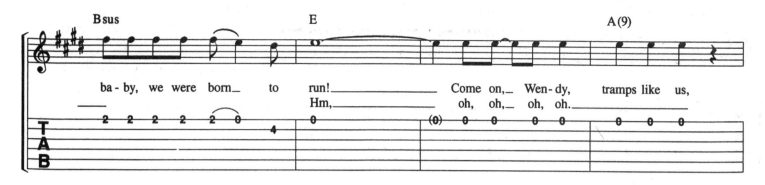

Verse 2:
Wendy, let me in,
I wanna be your friend,
I wanna guard your dreams and visions.
Just wrap your legs 'round these
Velvet rims and strap your hands
'Cross my engines.

Pre-Chorus 2:
Together we could break this trap.
We'll run till we drop,
And, baby, we'll never look back.
Oh, will you walk with me
Out on the wire?
'Cause baby, I'm just a scared
And lonely rider,
But I gotta know if love is wild,
Babe, I want to know if love is real.
(To Chorus:)

Verse 3:
The highway's jammed with broken heroes
On a last chance power drive.
Ev'rybody's out on the run tonight,
But there's no place left to hide.

Pre-Chorus 3:
Together, Wendy, we can live
With the sadness.
I'll love you with all the
Madness in my soul.
Oh, someday, girl,
I don't know when,
We're gonna get to that place where
We really wanna go,
And we'll walk in the sun.
But till then,
Tramps like us,
Baby, we were born to run.
(To Chorus:)

BLACK DOG

Words and Music by
JIMMY PAGE, ROBERT PLANT
and JOHN PAUL JONES

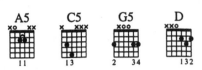

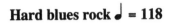

Hard blues rock ♩ = 118

Verses 1 & 3:

1. Hey, hey ma - ma, said the way you move, ___ gon - na
(3.) take too long ___ 'fore I found out ___ what

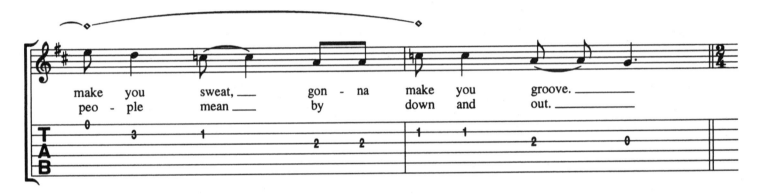

make you sweat, ___ gon - na make you groove. ___
peo - ple mean ___ by down and out. ___

Gtr. 1 N.C.

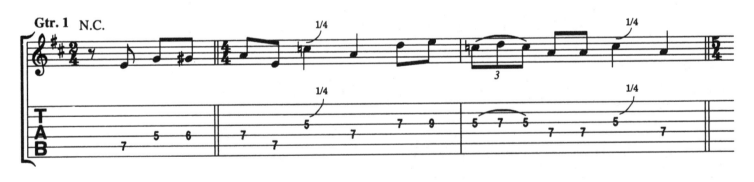

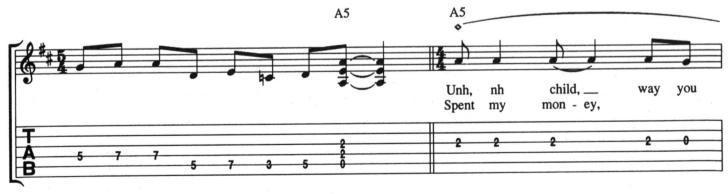

Unh, nh child, ___ way you
Spent my mon - ey,

Black Dog - 6 - 1

Black Dog - 6 - 2

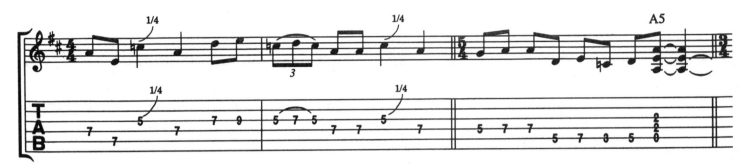

Chorus:

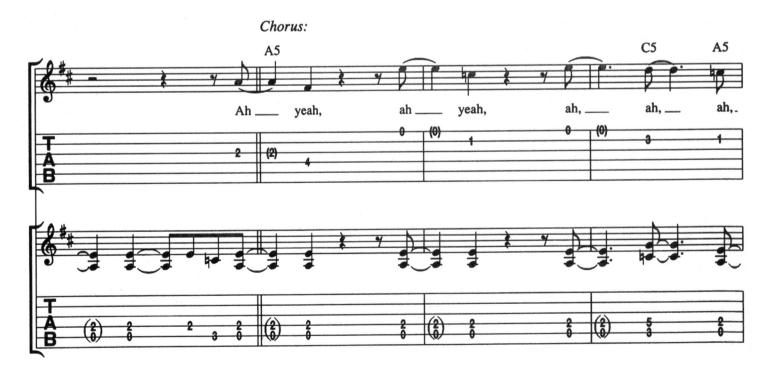

Verses 2 & 4:

2. I got-ta roll, can't stand still, __ got-ta flame-in' heart, __ can't
4. All I ask __ for, all I pray, _____ stead-y load-ed wom-an gon-na

get my ___ fill.
come my ___ way.

28

Eyes that shine, ___ burn-in' red, ___ dreams of you ___ all through my head.
Need a wom-an gon-na hold my hand, ___ will tell me no lies, ___ make me a hap-py man.

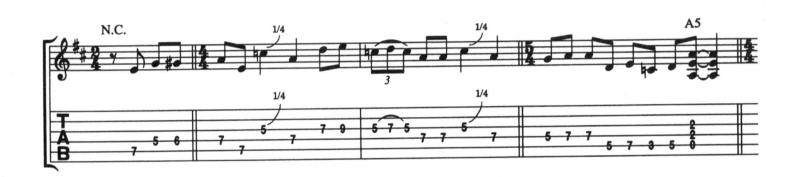

Bridge:

Ah ah ah ah ah ah ah ah ah ah ah ah

Chorus:

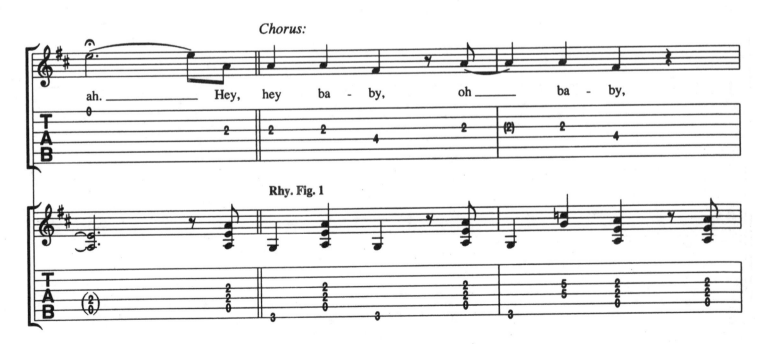

ah. _____ Hey, hey ba - by, oh _____ ba - by,

Rhy. Fig. 1

BORN IN THE U.S.A.

Words and Music by
BRUCE SPRINGSTEEN

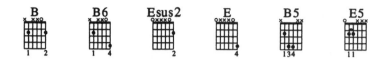

32

BORN ON THE BAYOU

Words and Music by
JOHN C. FOGERTY

Born on the Bayou - 4 - 4

CAN'T CRY ANYMORE

Words and Music by
SHERYL CROW and BILL BOTTRELL

Can't Cry Anymore - 4 - 1

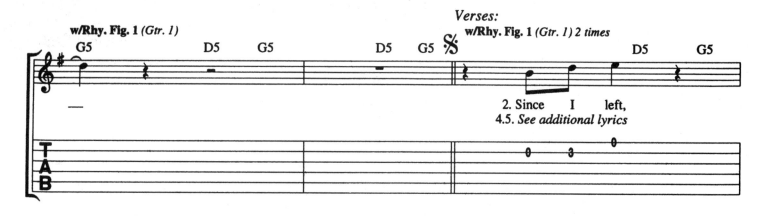

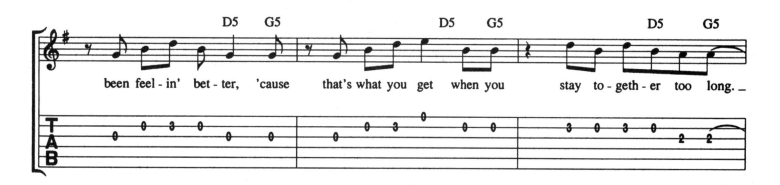

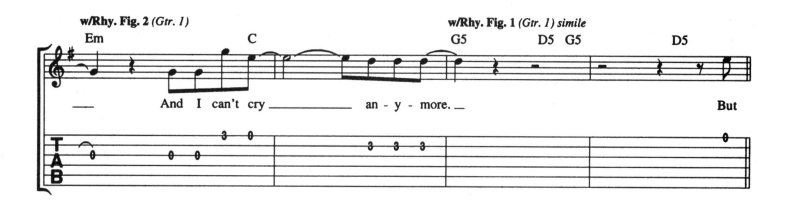

Can't Cry Anymore - 4 - 2

Verse 3:
And now I know that
Money comes in,
But the fact is (there's)
Not enough to pay my taxes.
And I can't cry anymore.
(To Chorus:)

Verse 4:
Well, gotta brother.
He's got real problems.
Heroin now,
There's just no stopping him tonight.
And I won't cry anymore.
(To Chorus:)

Verse 5:
Well, it could be worse.
I could've missed my calling.
Sometimes it hurts,
But when you read the writing on the wall,
Can't cry anymore.
(To Chorus:)

CASEY JONES

Words by
ROBERT HUNTER
Music by
JERRY GARCIA

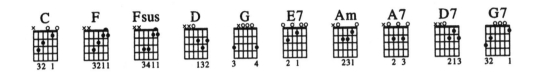

Medium tempo
Intro:
Rhy. Fig. 1

(Gtr. 2 to rhy. slashes)

Chorus:

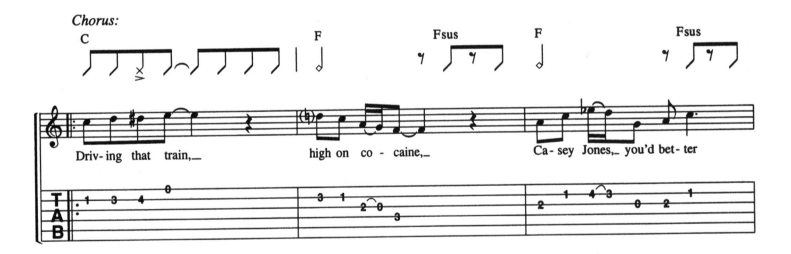

Driv-ing that train,____ high on co - caine,____ Ca-sey Jones,_ you'd bet- ter

Cont. rhy. simile

watch your speed.____ Trou - ble a - head,____ trou-ble be - hind,____

Casey Jones - 4 - 1

44

Verse 3:
Trouble with you is the trouble with me,
Got two good eyes but we still don't see.
Come 'round the bend, you know it's the end.
The fireman screams and the engine just gleams.

CHINA GROVE

Words and Music by
TOM JOHNSTON

48

though it's a part of the Lone Star State, _ peo - ple don't seem _ to care; _

they just keep on look - in' to the east.

Gtr. 2

China Grove - 6 - 4

50

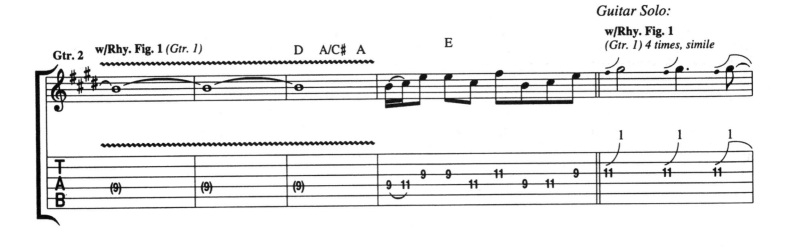

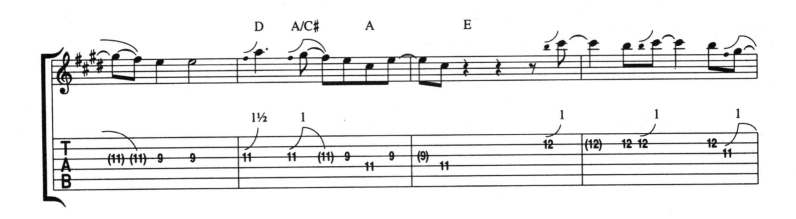

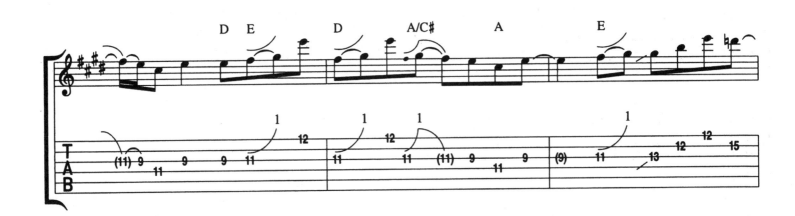

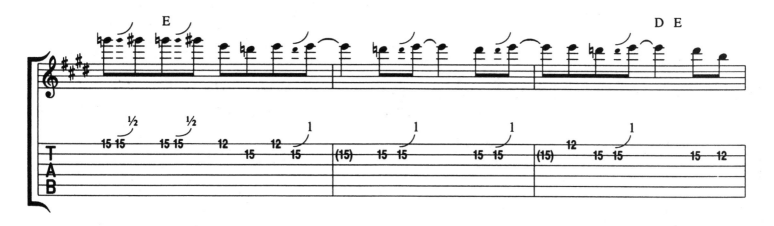

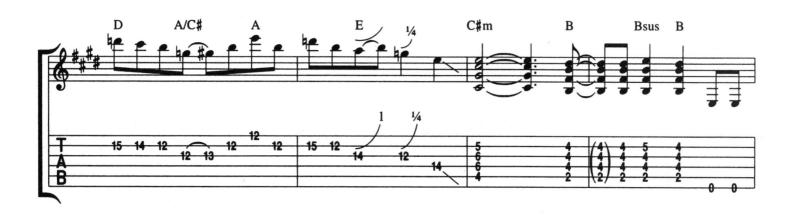

Verse 2:
Well, the preacher and the teacher, Lord, they're a caution,
They are the talk of the town.
When the gossip gets to flyin' and they ain't lyin'
When the sun goes fallin' down.

Pre-Chorus 2:
They say that the father's insane,
And dear Missus Perkin's a game.
(To Chorus:)

COPPERLINE

Words and Music by
JAMES TAYLOR and REYNOLDS PRICE

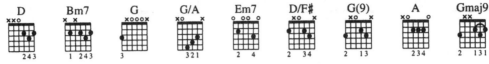

All gtrs. capo at 2nd fret to match recording

Moderately

Verses:

1. E-ven the old folks nev-er knew
2.4. *See additional lyrics*

why they call it like they do. I was won-d'ring since the

54

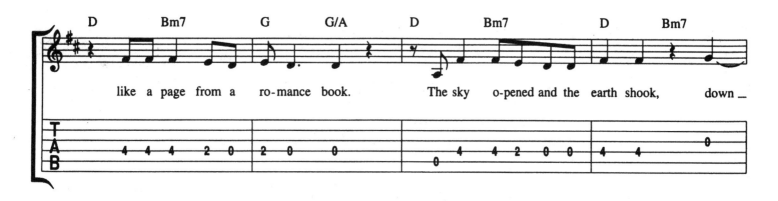

like a page from a ro-mance book. The sky o-pened and the earth shook, down

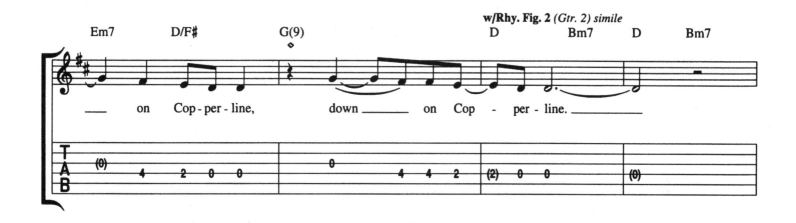

on Cop-per-line, down on Cop - per - line.

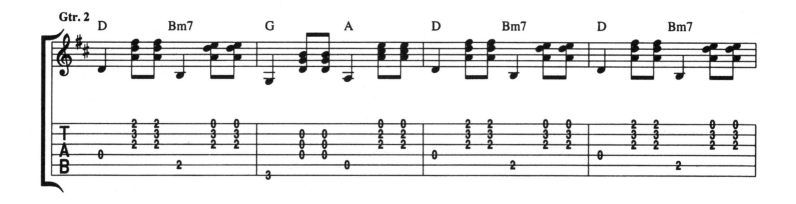

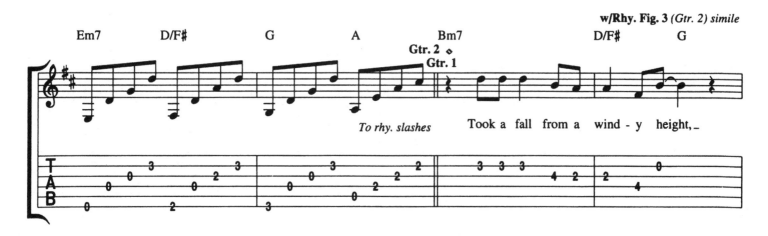

To rhy. slashes   Took a fall from a wind-y height,

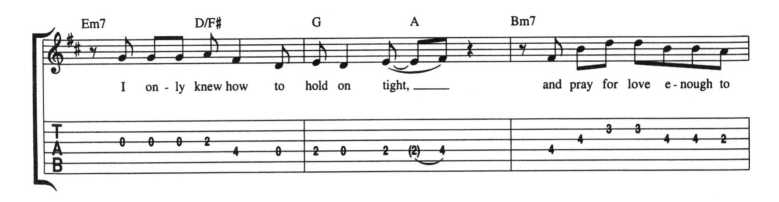

I on-ly knew how to hold on tight, ___ and pray for love e-nough to

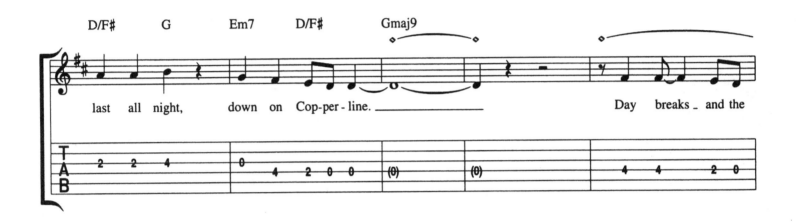

last all night, down on Cop-per-line. ___ Day breaks _ and the

boy wakes up, and the dog barks, _ and the bird sings, _ and the

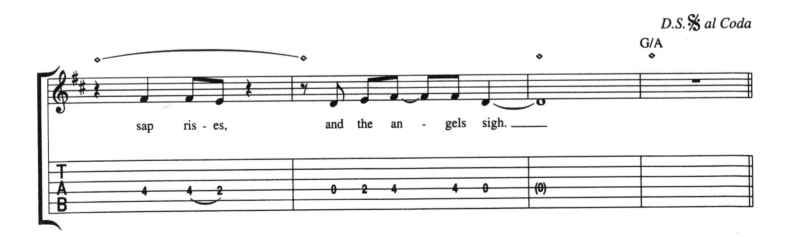

D.S. 𝄋 *al Coda*

sap ris-es, and the an-gels sigh. ___

57

Verse 2:
Warm summer night on the Copperline,
Slip away past supper time.
Wood smoke and moonshine,
Down on Copperline.
One time, I saw my daddy dance,
Watched him moving like a man in a trance.
He brought it back from the war in France,
Down onto Copperline.

Chorus 2:
Branch water and tomato wine,
Creosote and turpentine.
Sour mash and new moonshine,
Down on Copperline,
We were down on Copperline.
(To Verse 3:)

Verse 4:
I tried to go back, as if I could.
All spec house and plywood.
Tore up and love up good,
Down on Copperline.
It doesn't come as a surprise to me,
It doesn't touch my memory.
Man, I'm lifting up and rising free,
Down over Copperline.
(To Chorus:)

Copperline - 6 - 6

DESPERADO

Words and Music by
DON HENLEY and GLENN FREY

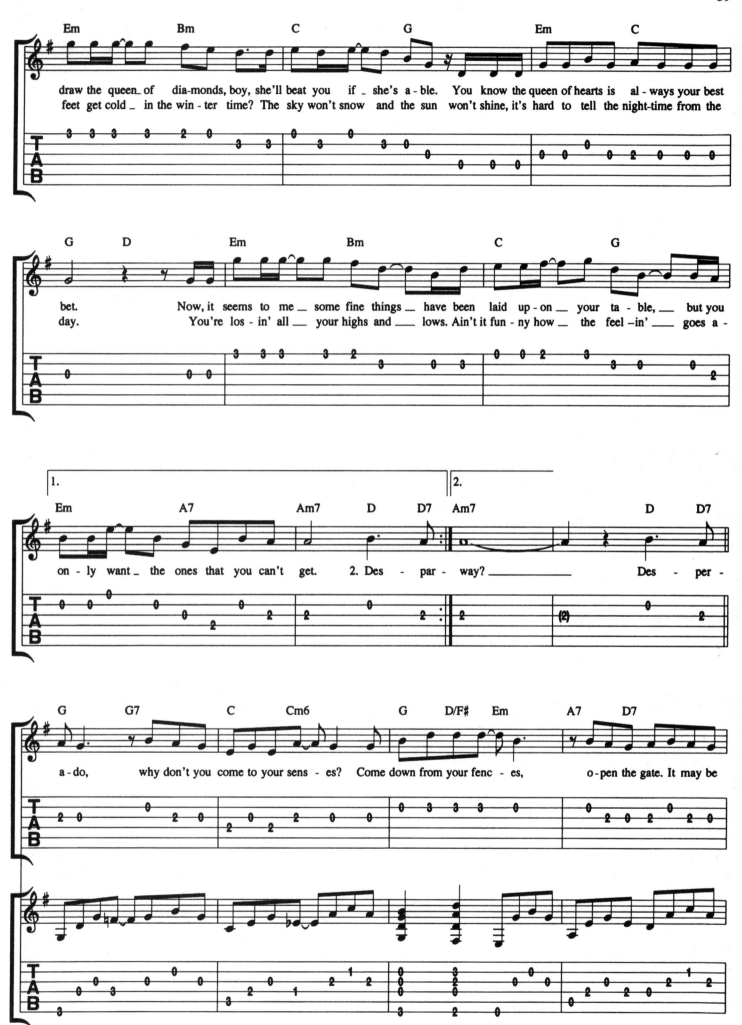

rain - in', but there's a rain - bow a - bove ___ you. You bet - ter let some - bod - y love you.

You bet - ter let some - bod - y love you be - fore it's too ___

late.

FORTUNATE SON

Words and Music by
JOHN C. FOGERTY

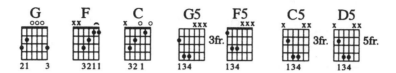

Fortunate Son - 3 - 1

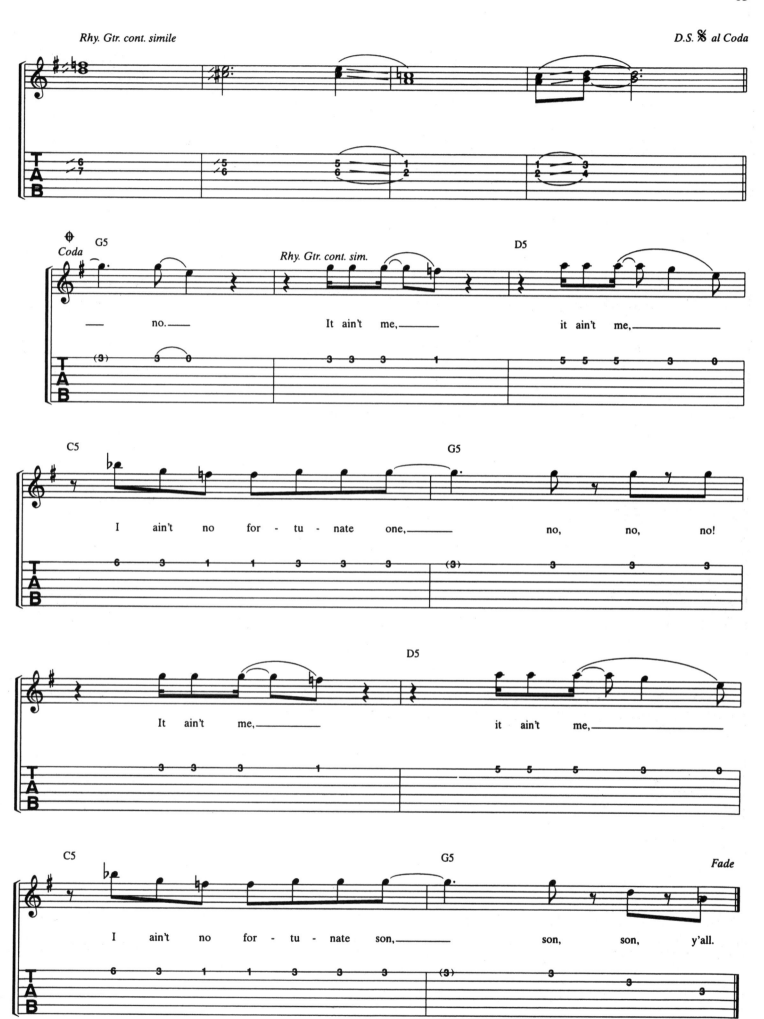

DOWN ON THE CORNER

Words and Music by
JOHN C. FOGERTY

Down on the Corner - 4 - 1

Down on the Corner - 4 - 2

Down on the Corner - 4 - 3

EARLY MORNIN' RAIN

Words and Music by
GORDON LIGHTFOOT

All gtrs. capo 3rd fret to match recording.

Early Mornin' Rain - 4 - 1

Verse 3:
Hear the mighty engines roar,
See the silver bird on high;
She's away and westward bound.
Far above the clouds she'll fly,
Where the mornin' rain don't fall
And the sun always shines.
She'll be flying o'er my home,
In about three hours time.

Verse 4:
This old airport's got me down;
It's no earthly good to me.
And I'm stuck here on the ground,
As cold and drunk as I can be.
You can't jump a jet plane
Like you can a freight train;
So, I'd best be on my way
In the early mornin' rain.

EVERYDAY IS A WINDING ROAD

Words and Music by
SHERYL CROW, BRIAN MacLEOD
and JEFF TROTT

Everyday Is a Winding Road - 6 - 1

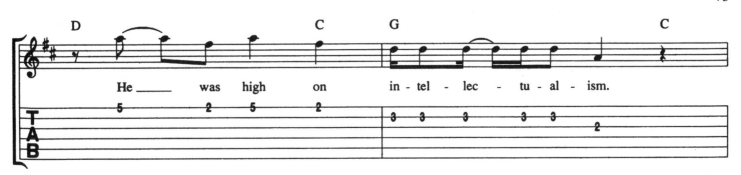

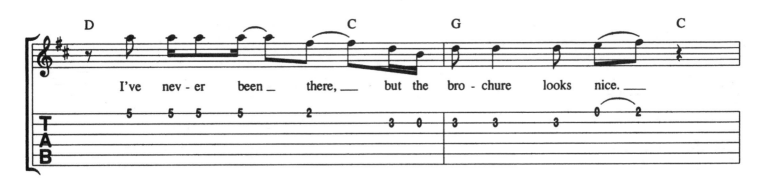

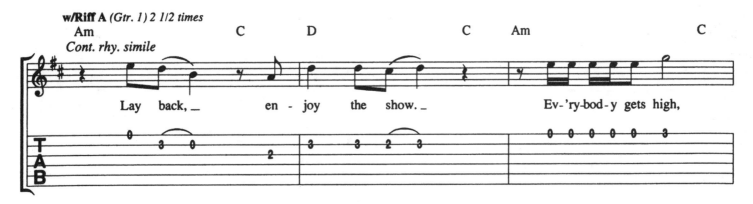

Verse 2:
He's got a daughter he calls Easter,
She was born on a Tuesday night.
I'm just wondering why I feel so all alone,
Why I'm a stranger in my own life.
(To Pre-Chorus:)

FRIEND OF THE DEVIL

Words by
ROBERT HUNTER
Music by
JERRY GARCIA and JOHN DAWSON

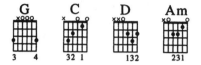

Moderately fast
Intro:
Rhy. Fig. 1

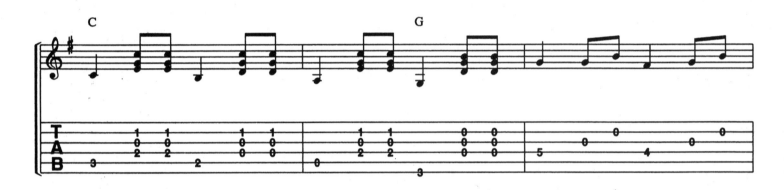

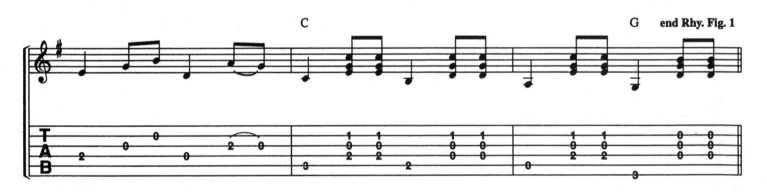

1. I lit out__ from Re - no, I__ was trailed__ by twen-ty hounds.__
(2.) ran in - to the dev - il, babe,__ he loaned__ me twen-ty bills.__ He
3. *See additional lyrics*

Friend of the Devil - 4 - 2

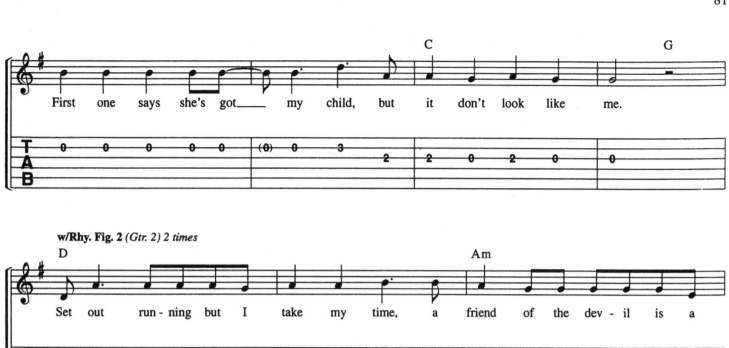

First one says she's got___ my child, but it don't look like me.

w/Rhy. Fig. 2 *(Gtr. 2) 2 times*

Set out run-ning but I take my time, a friend of the dev-il is a

friend of mine.___ If I get some__ be-fore___ day-light,___ just might get some

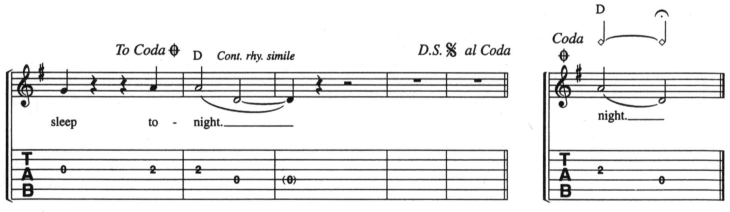

To Coda ⊕ *Cont. rhy. simile* D.S. 𝄋 *al Coda* *Coda*

sleep to - night.___ night.___

Verse 3:
I ran down to the levee,
But the devil caught me there.
He took my twenty dollar bill
And he vanished in the air.
(To Bridge:)

Friend of the Devil - 4 - 4

GO YOUR OWN WAY

Words and Music by
LINDSEY BUCKINGHAM

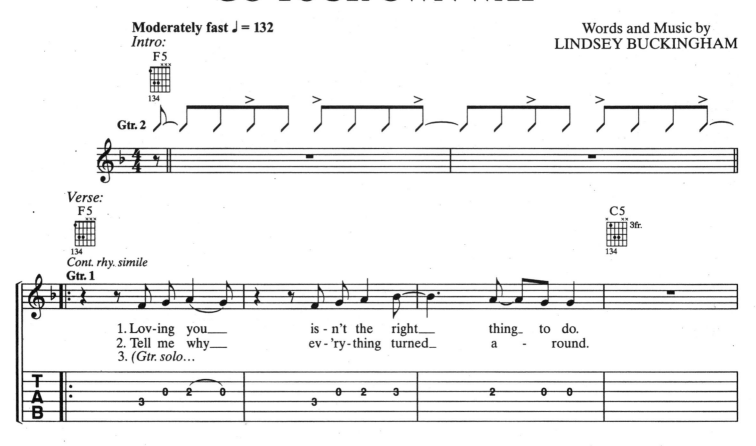

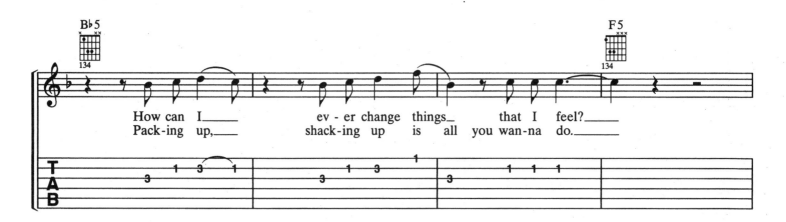

Go Your Own Way - 3 - 1

Go Your Own Way - 3 - 2

GOING DOWN THE ROAD FEELIN' BAD

Trad., Arrangement by
GRATEFUL DEAD

HARVEST MOON

Words and Music by
NEIL YOUNG

Harvest Moon - 5 - 1

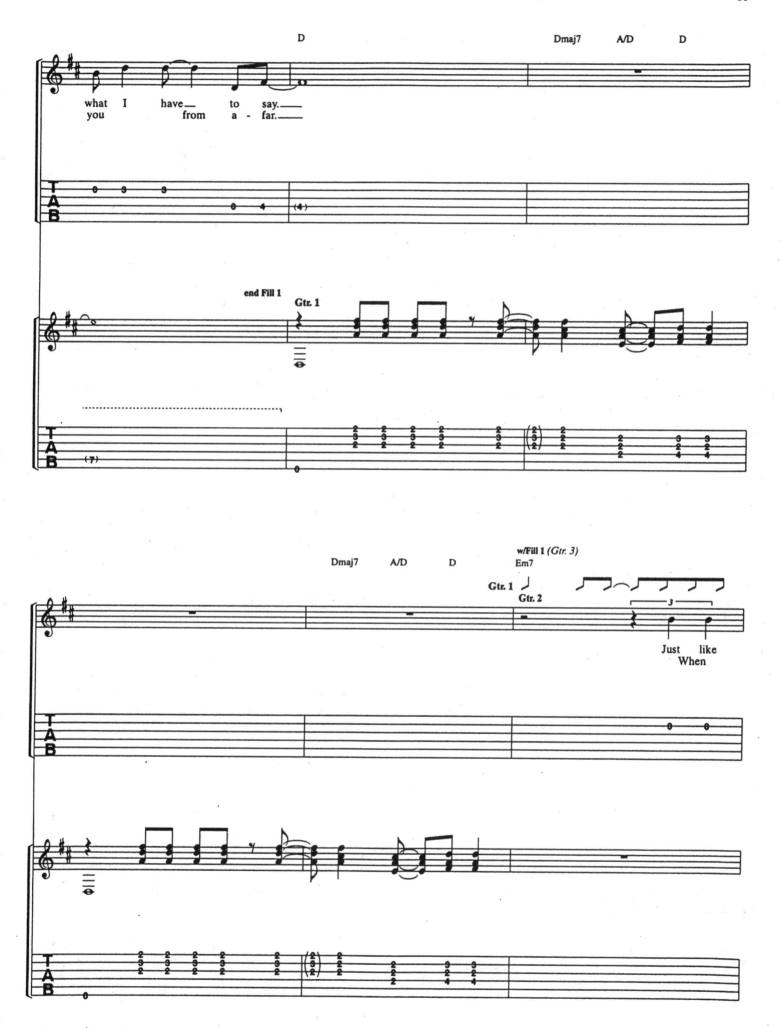

Harvest Moon - 5 - 2

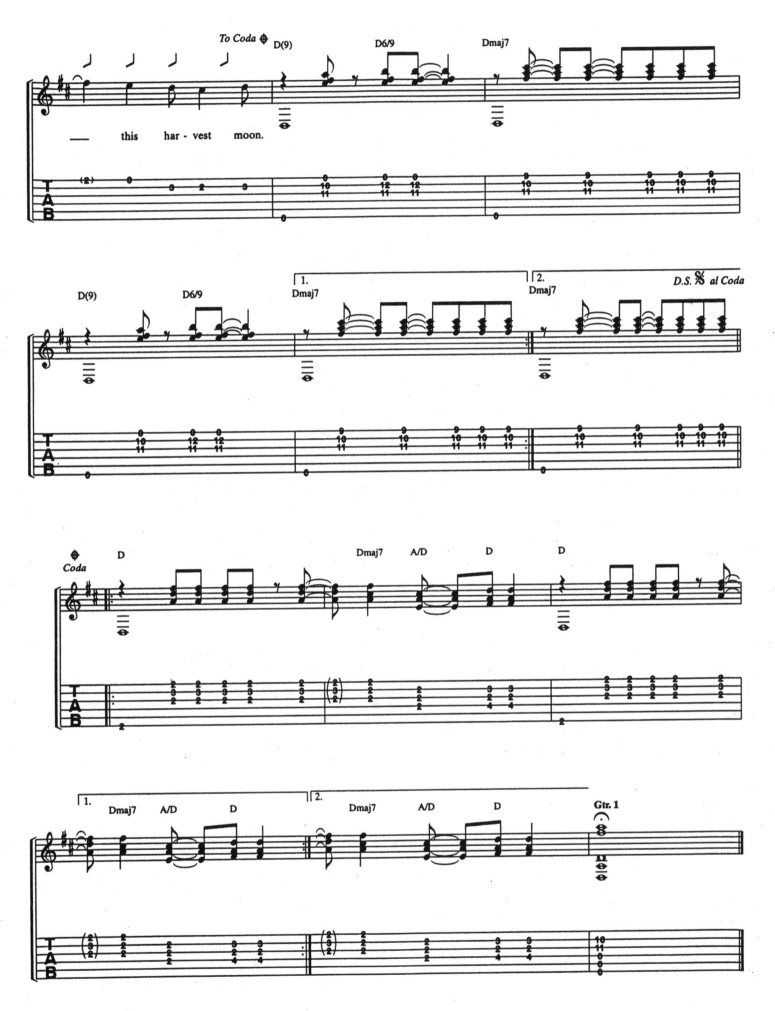

I NEED YOU

Words and Music by
GERRY BECKLEY

I Need You - 3 - 1

left to me,___   left to me.___   I need___ you   like the flow-

- er needs_ the rain,_ you know_ I need_ you.   Guess I'll start it all_ a - gain,_ you know_ I need_

___ you.   Like the win - ter needs_ the spring,_ you know_ I need_ you,   I need

you.   2. And   ev - 'ry day_   I'd laugh the

HEART OF GOLD

Words and Music by
NEIL YOUNG

Heart of Gold - 2 - 2

A HORSE WITH NO NAME

Words and Music by
DEWEY BUNNELL

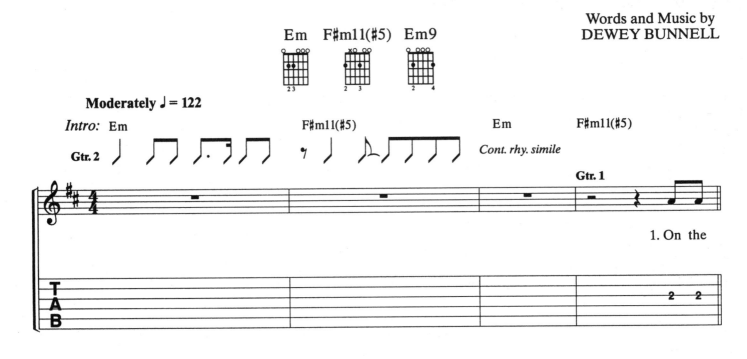

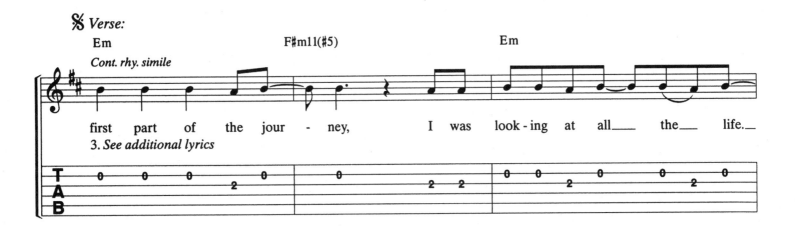

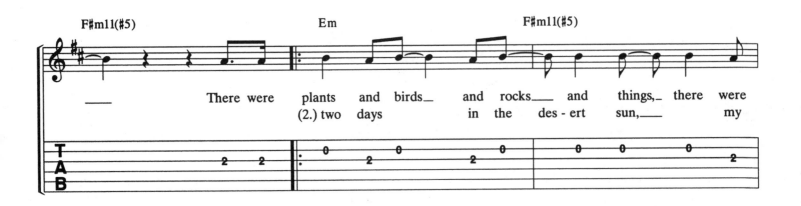

A Horse With No Name - 4 - 1

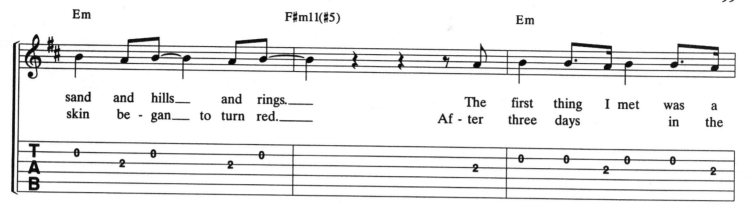

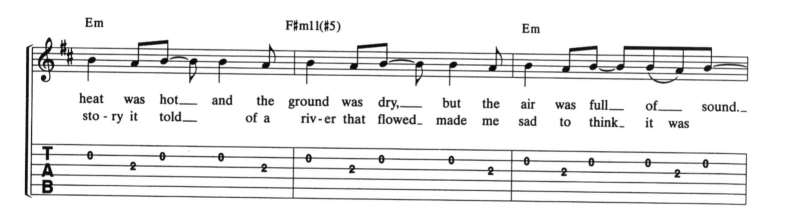

A Horse With No Name - 4 - 2

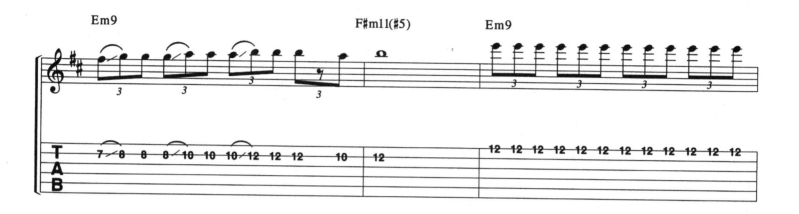

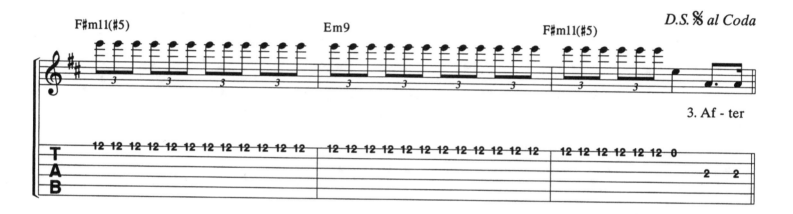

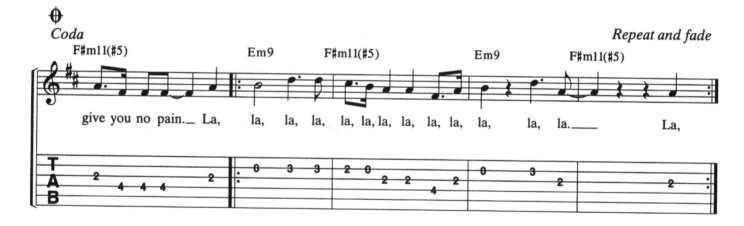

Verse 3:
After nine days, I let the horse run free,
'Cause the desert had turned to sea.
There were plants and birds and rocks and things,
There was sand and hills and rings.
The ocean is a desert with its life underground
And the perfect disguise above.
Under the cities lies a heart made of ground,
But the humans will give no love.
(To Chorus:)

HOTEL CALIFORNIA

Words and Music by
DON HENLEY, GLENN FREY
and DON FELDER

Gtr. 1 with capo at 7th fret

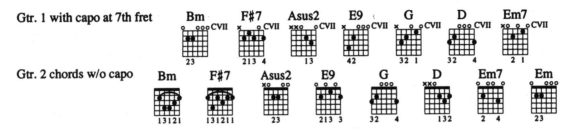

Gtr. 2 chords w/o capo

Moderately ♩ = 74

Intro:

Gtr. 1*

Rhy. Fig. 1

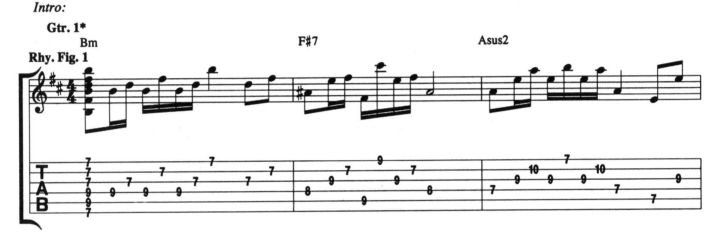

* Capo at VII fret. Number 7 in tab represents capoed open string

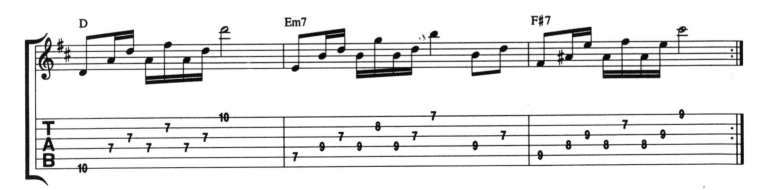

Hotel California - 6 - 1

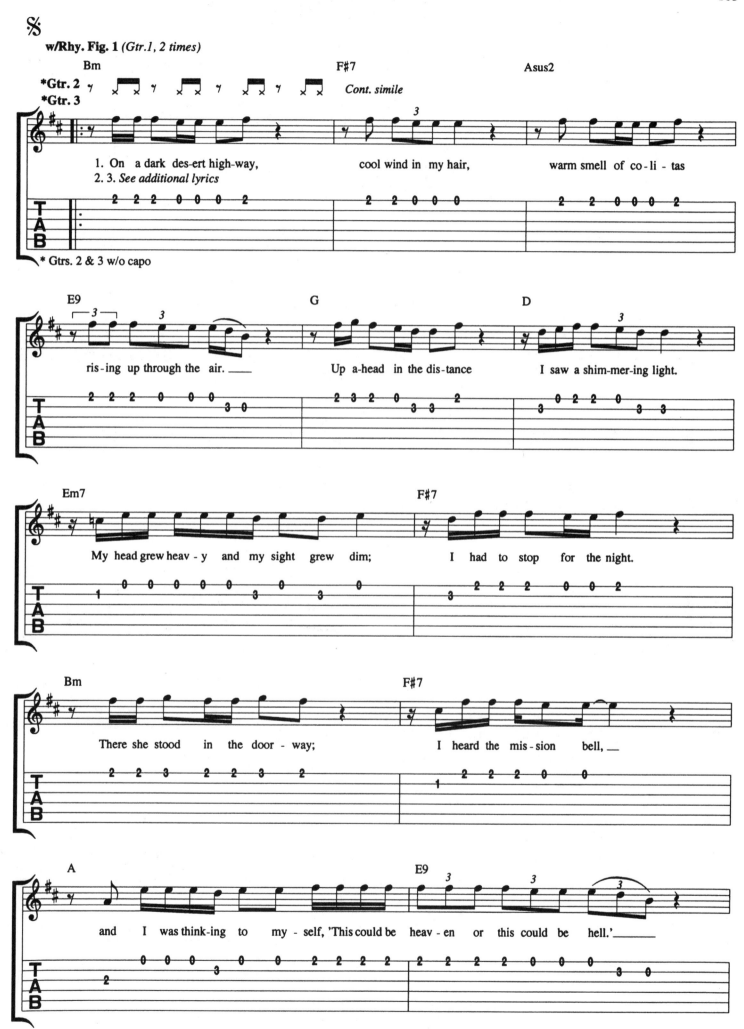

Hotel California - 6 - 4

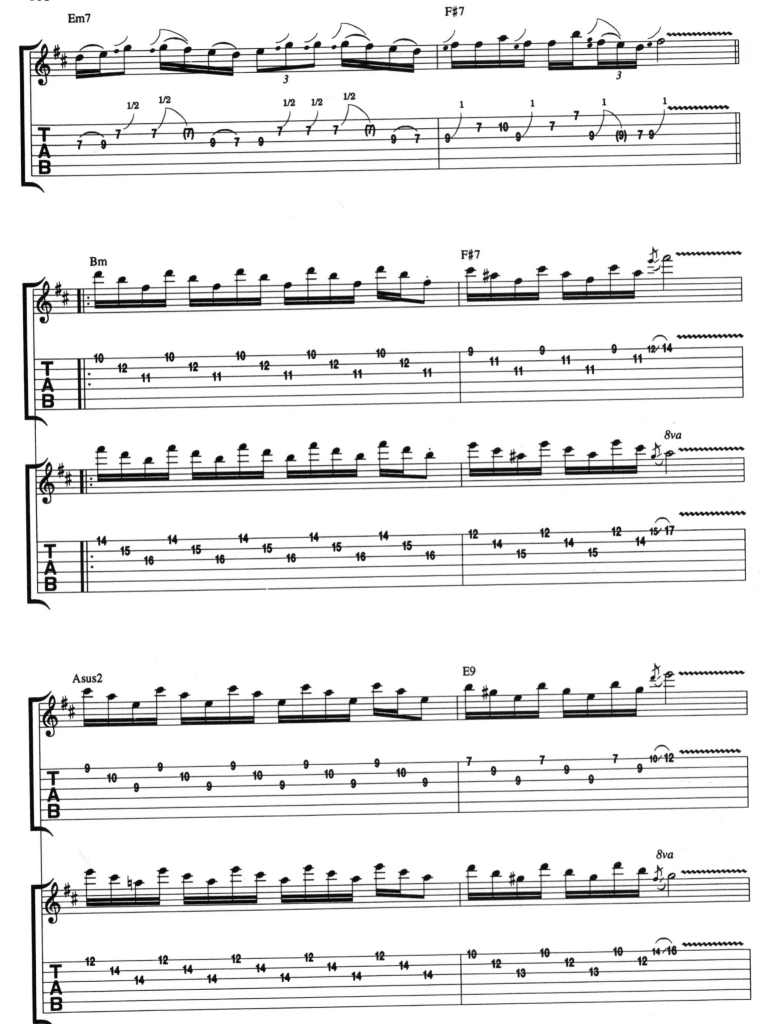

Repeat & fade

Verse 2:

Her mind is Tiffany twisted.
She got her Mercedes Bends.
She got a lot of pretty, pretty boys
That she calls friends.
How they dance in the courtyard;
Sweet summer sweat.
Some dance to remember;
Some dance to forget.
So I called up the captain:
"Please bring me my wine."
He said, "We haven't had that spirit here
Since nineteen sixty nine."
And still those voices are calling from far away;
Wake you up in the middle of the night
Just to hear them say:

(To Chorus:)

Verse 3:

Mirrors on the ceiling,
The pink champagne on ice,
And she said, "We are all just prisoners here
Of our own device."
And in the master's chambers,
They gathered for the feast.
They stab it with their steely knives,
But they just can't kill the beast.
Last thing I remember,
I was running for the door.
I had to find the passage back
To the place I was before.
"Relax," said the night man.
"We are progammed to receive.
You can check out any time you like,
But you can never leave."

(To Guitar Solo:)

I'M ON FIRE

Words and Music by
BRUCE SPRINGSTEEN

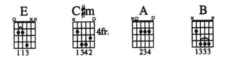

I'm on Fire - 4 - 1

110

I'm on Fire - 4 - 3

Verse 2:
Tell me now, baby, is he good to you?
Can he do to you the things that I do?
I can take you higher.
Oh, I'm on fire!

Verse 3:
At night, I wake up with the sheets soaking wet
And a freight train running through the middle of my head.
Only you can cool my desire.
Oh, I'm on fire!

I'm on Fire - 4 - 4

IF IT MAKES YOU HAPPY

Words and Music by
SHERYL CROW and JEFF TROTT

If It Makes You Happy - 5 - 1

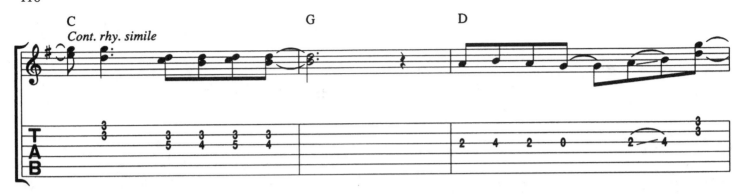

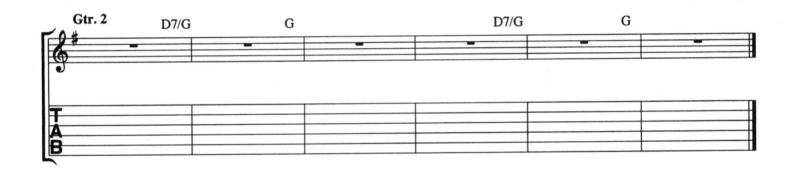

Verse 3:
You get down, real low down.
You listen to Coltrane, derail your own train.
Well, who hasn't been there before?

Verse 4:
I come 'round, around the hard way.
Bring your comics in bed, scrape the mold off the bread,
And serve you French toast again.

Pre-Chorus 2:
Well, okay, I still get stoned.
I'm not the kind of girl you'd take home.
(To Chorus:)

Verse 5:
We've been far, far away from here.
Put on a poncho, played for mosquitoes,
And everywhere in between.

Pre-Chorus 3:
Well, o.k., we get along.
So what if right now everything's wrong?
(To Chorus:)

LISTEN TO THE MUSIC

Words and Music by
TOM JOHNSTON

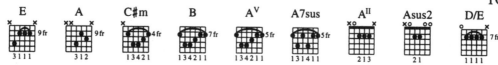

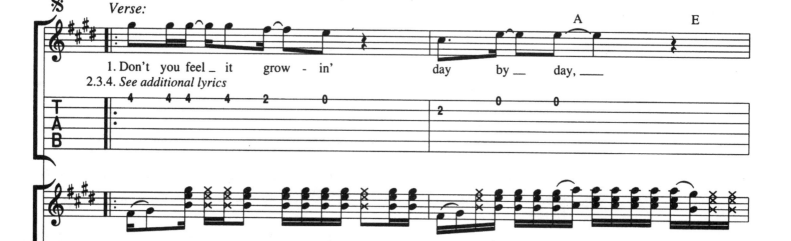

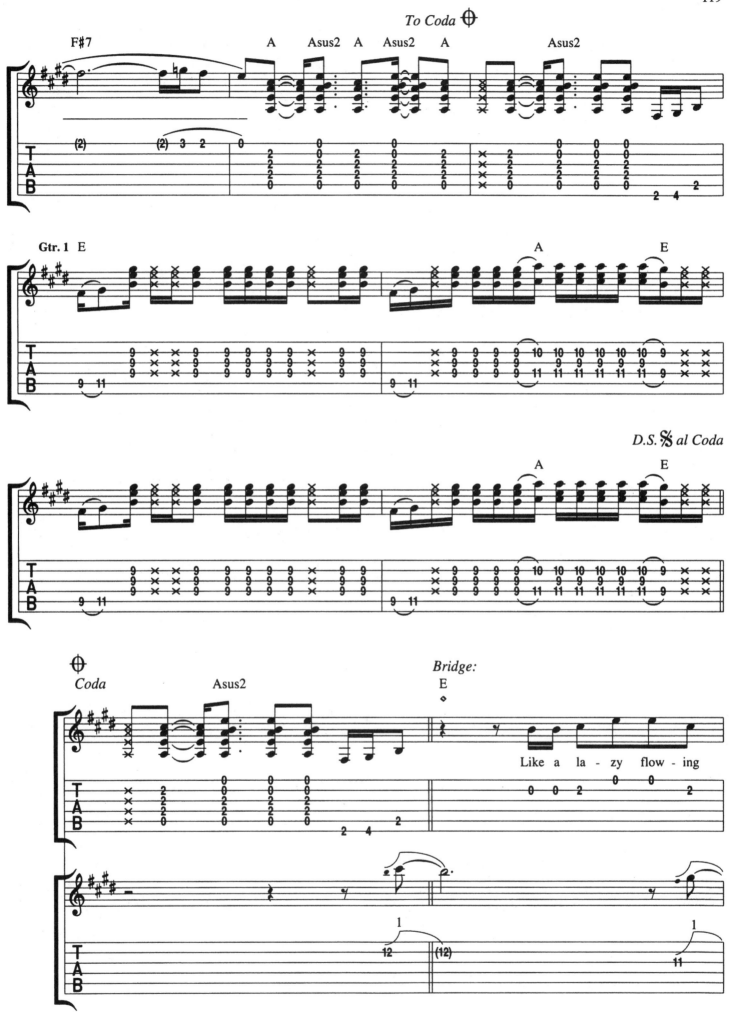

120

Outro Chorus:

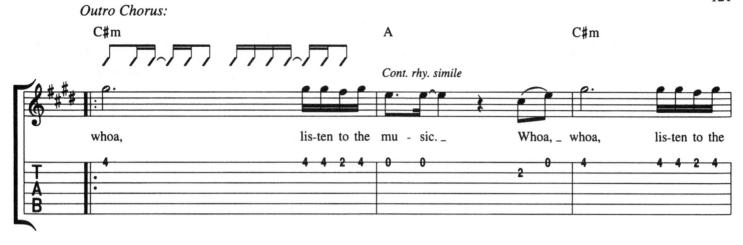

whoa, lis-ten to the mu - sic. _ Whoa, _ whoa, lis-ten to the

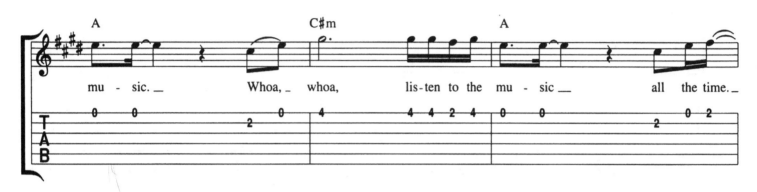

mu - sic. _ Whoa, _ whoa, lis-ten to the mu - sic _ all the time. _

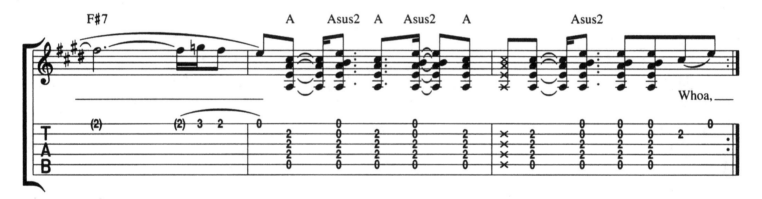

Whoa, ___

Verse 2:
What the people need is a way to make 'em smile.
It ain't so hard to do if you know how.
Gotta get a message, get it on through.
Oh, now mama's goin' to after 'while.
(To Chorus:)

Verse 3:
Well, I know you know better,
Everything I say,
Meet me in the country for a day.
We'll be happy and we'll dance,
Oh, we're gonna dance our blues away.

Verse 4:
And if I'm feeling good to you,
And you're feelin' good to me,
There ain't nothin' we can't do or say,
Feelin' good, feelin' fine.
Oh, baby, let the music play.
(To Chorus:)

IF YOU COULD READ MY MIND

All gtrs. capo 2nd fret to match recording.

Words and Music by
GORDON LIGHTFOOT

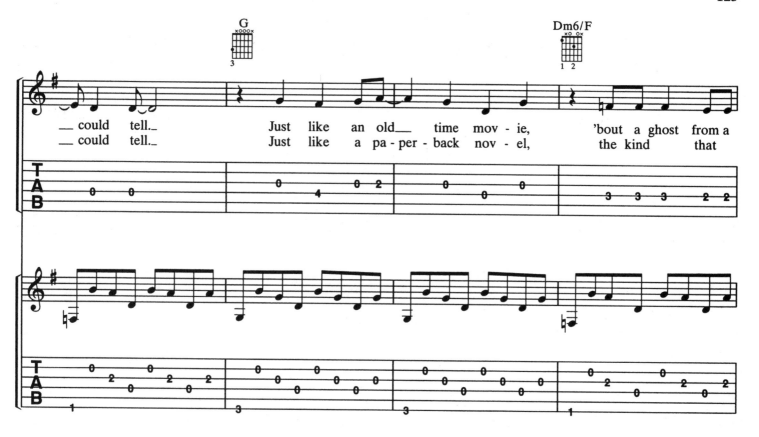

that you can't see.
too hard to take.

126

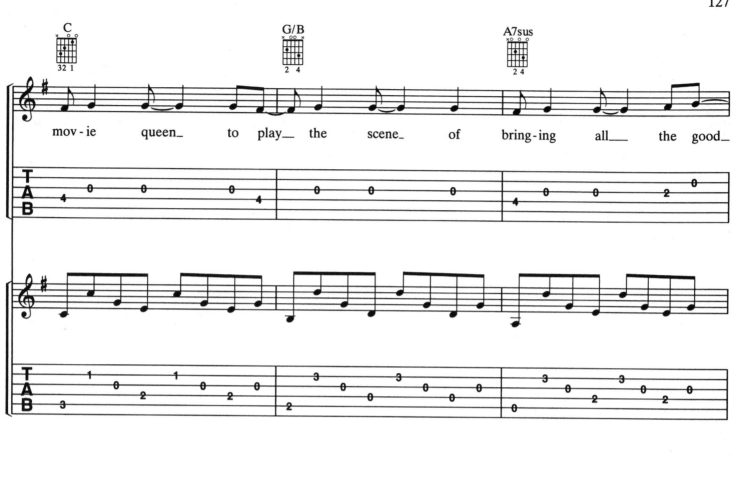

128

D.S.℅ al Coda

Coda

I don't know_ where we_ went wrong,_ but the feel-in's gone_ and I

just can't get it back.

But sto-ries_ al-ways end,_ and if you read_ be-tween_

_ the lines,_ you'll know that I'm_ just try-in' to un-der-stand_ the

If You Could Read My Mind - 8 - 7

JUMP

Words and Music by
EDWARD VAN HALEN, ALEX VAN HALEN
and DAVID LEE ROTH

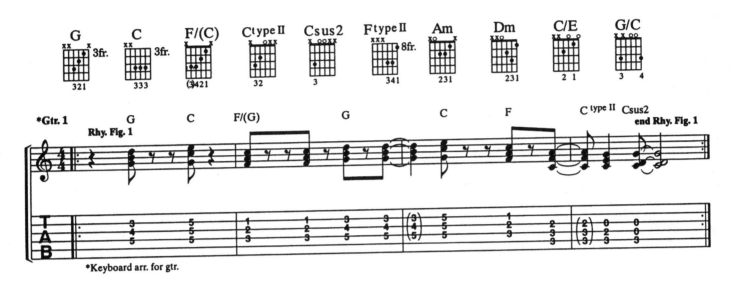

*Keyboard arr. for gtr.

I get up—

and noth-ing gets me— down.— You get it

Jump - 4 - 1

Jump - 4 - 2

Might as well jump.—

Chorus:
w/Rhy. Fig. 1 *(Gtr. 1, 2 times)*

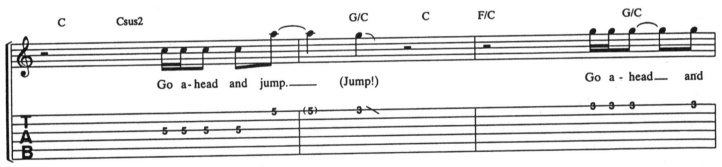

(Jump!)   Might as well jump.—

Go a-head and jump.— (Jump!)   Go a-head and

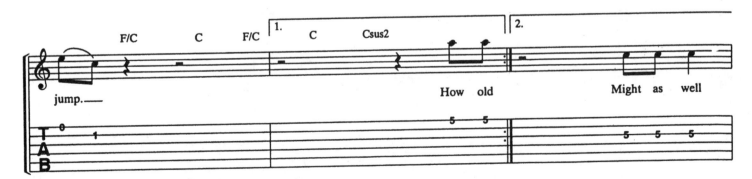

jump.—   How old   Might as well

LONELY PEOPLE

Words and Music by
DAN PEEK and CATHERINE L. PEEK

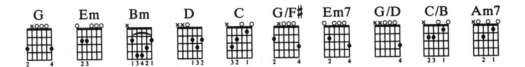

Moderately fast ♩ = 152

Intro:

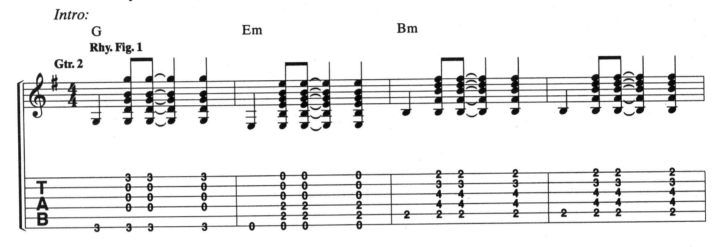

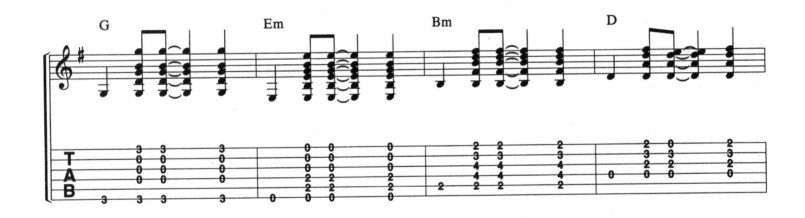

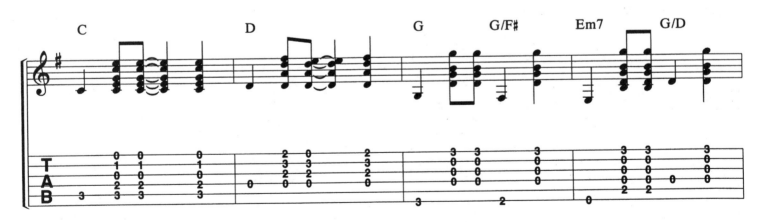

Lonely People - 3 - 1

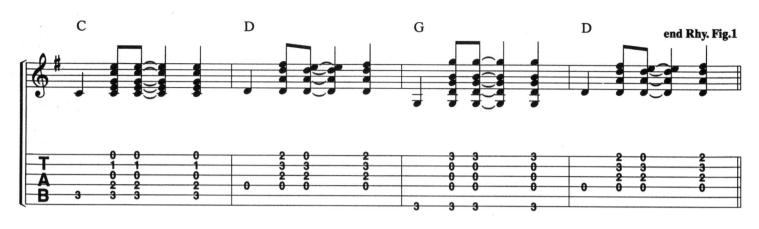

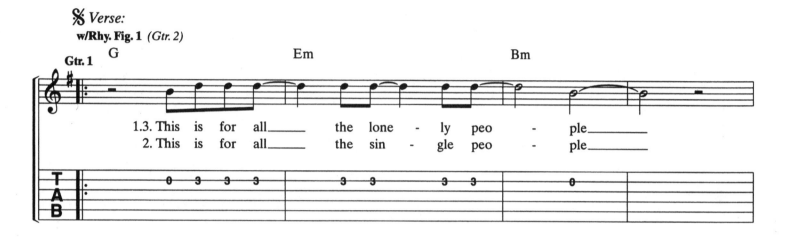

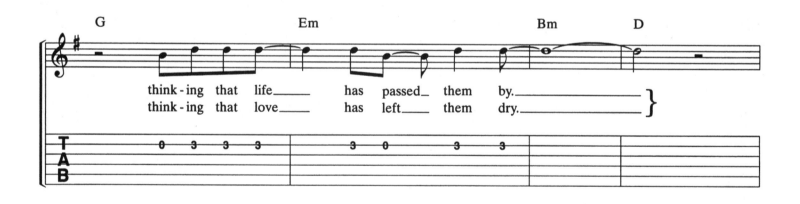

LONG TRAIN RUNNIN'

Words and Music by
TOM JOHNSTON

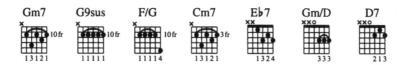

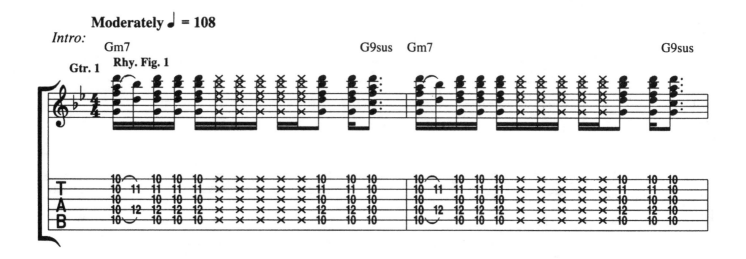

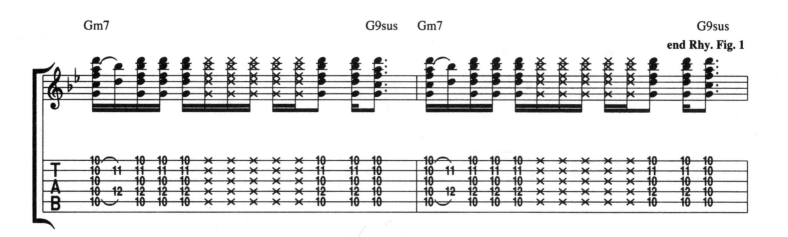

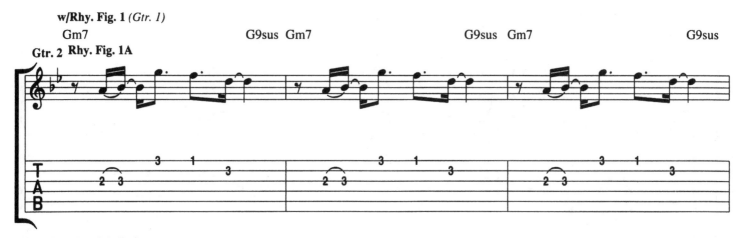

Long Train Runnin' - 5 - 1

Verses:

w/Rhy. Figs. 1 *(Gtr. 1)* **& 1A** *(Gtr. 2) Verses 1, 2 & 4 only*
w/Rhy. Fig. 2 *(Gtrs. 1 & 2) Verses 3 & 5 only*
w/Rhy. Fig. 3 *(Gtrs. 1 & 2) Verse 6 only*

1. Down a-round_ the cor-ner,   half a mile_ from here,_   you

2. – 6. *See additional lyrics*

see them old trains run - nin', and you watch them dis - ap - pear._   With-out

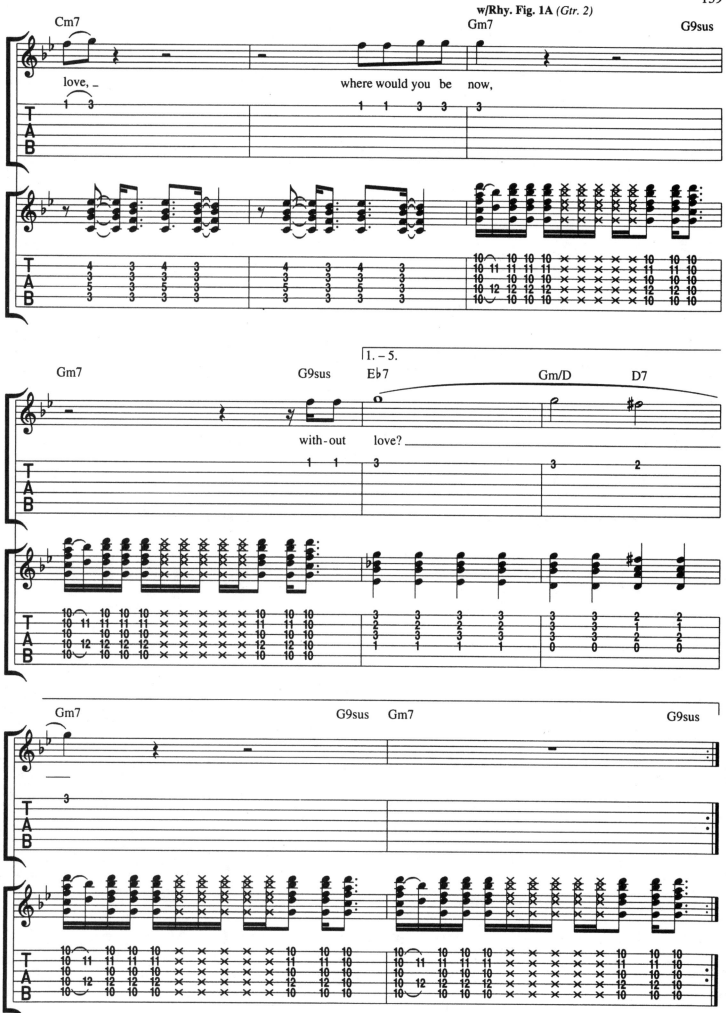

140

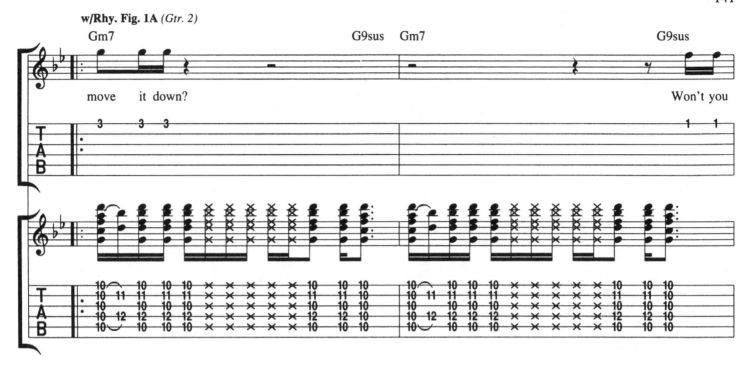

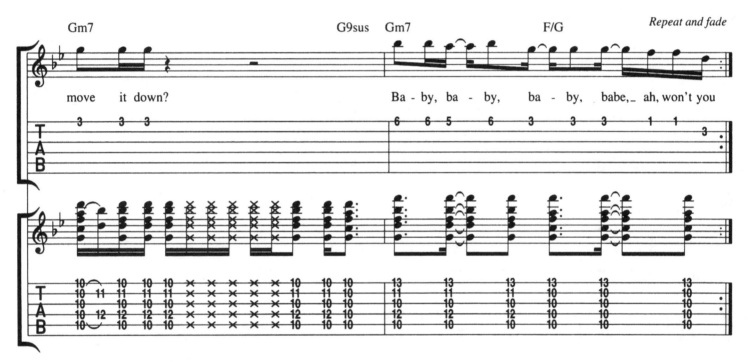

Verse 2:
You know I saw Miss Lucy,
Down along the tracks;
She lost her home and her family,
And she won't be comin' back.
Without love, where would you be right now,
Without love?
(To Verse 3:)

Verses 3 & 5:
Well, the Illinois Central
And the Southern Central freight
Gotta keep on pushin', mama,
'Cause you know they're runnin' late.
Without love, where would you be now,
Without love?
(1st time to Verse 4:)
(2nd time to Verse 6:)

Verse 4:
Harmonica Solo:
(To Verse 5:)

Verse 6:
Where pistons keep on churnin'
And the wheels go 'round and 'round,
And the steel rails are cold and hard
For the miles that they go down.
Without love, where would you be right now,
Without love?
(To Coda)

LYIN' EYES

Words and Music by
DON HENLEY and GLENN FREY

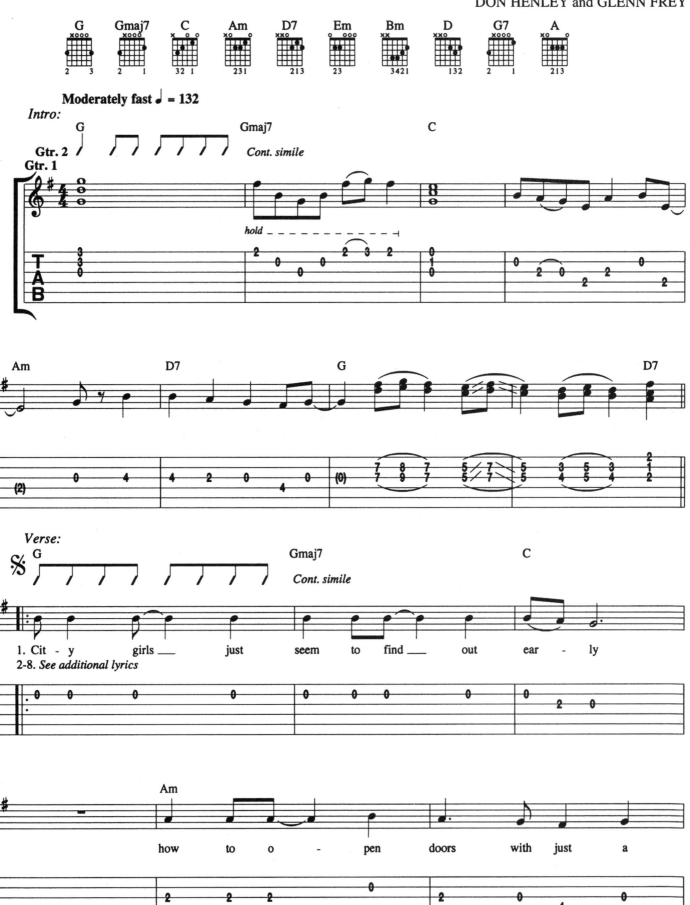

144

Verse 2:
Late at night her big old house gets lonely;
I guess every form of refuge has it's price.
And it breaks her heart to think her love is only
Given to a man with hands as cold as ice.

Verse 3:
So she tells him she must go out for the evening
To comfort an old friend who's feelin' down.
But he knows where she's goin' as she's leavin';
She is headed for the cheatin' side of town.
(To Chorus:)

Verse 4:
On the other side of town a boy is waiting
With firey eyes and dreams no one could steal.
She drives on through the night anticipating,
'Cause he makes her feel the way she used to feel.

Verse 5:
She rushes to his arms they fall together;
She whispers that it's only for a while.
She swears that soon she'll be coming back forever;
She pulls away and leaves him with a smile.
(To Chorus:)

Verse 6:
She gets up and pours herself a strong one
And stares out at the stars up in the sky.
Another night, it's gonna be a long one;
She draws the shade and hangs her head to cry.
(To Chorus:)

Verse 7:
She wonders how it ever got this crazy;
She thinks about a boy she knew in school.
Did she get tired or did she just get lazy,
She's so far gone she feels just like a fool.
(To Chorus:)

Verse 8:
My, oh my, you sure know how to arrange things;
You set it up so well, so carefully.
Ain't it funny how your new life didn't change things;
You're still the same old girl you used to be.
(To Chorus:)

MEXICO

Words and Music by
JAMES TAYLOR

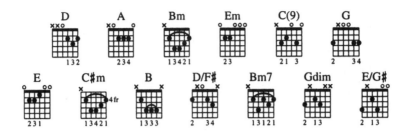

Moderately

Intro:

hold throughout

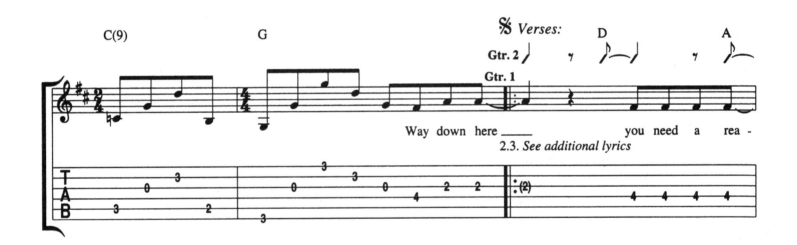

Way down here _____ you need a rea-

2.3. See additional lyrics

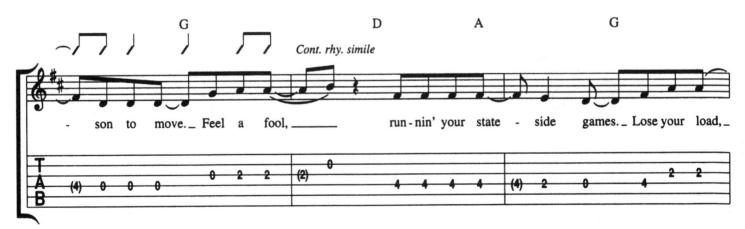

-son to move. _ Feel a fool, _____ run-nin' your state-side games. _ Lose your load, _

Mexico - 4 - 1

Mexico - 4 - 2

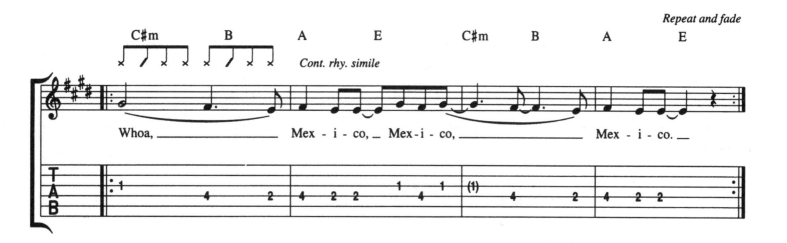

Verse 2:
America no got the sleepy eye,
But this body's still shakin' like a live wire.
Sleepy señorita with the eyes on fire.
(To Chorus:)

Verse 3:
Baby's hungry and the money's all gone.
The folks back home don't want to talk on the phone.
She gets a long letter, sends back a postcard; times are hard.

MY HOMETOWN

Words and Music by
BRUCE SPRINGSTEEN

My Hometown - 4 - 1

Verse 2:
In sixty-five, tension was running high at my high school;
There was lots of fights between the black and white, there was nothing you could do.
Two cars at a light, on a Saturday night; in a back seat, there was a gun.
Words were passed in a shotgun blast; troubled times had come...

Chorus 2:
To my hometown, my hometown, to my hometown, my homwtown...

Verse 3:
Last night me and Kate, we laid in bed, talking 'bout getting out,
Packing up our bags, maybe heading south.
I'm thirty-five, we got a boy of our own now.
Last night I sat him up, behind the wheel, and said, "Son, take a good look around,
This is your hometown."

NEVER GOING BACK AGAIN

All gtrs. capo at 4th fret
Gtr. 2 tuning:

Words and Music by
LINDSEY BUCKINGHAM

⑥ = D ③ = G
⑤ = A ② = B
④ = D ① = E

Never Going Back Again - 5 - 1

Instrumental:

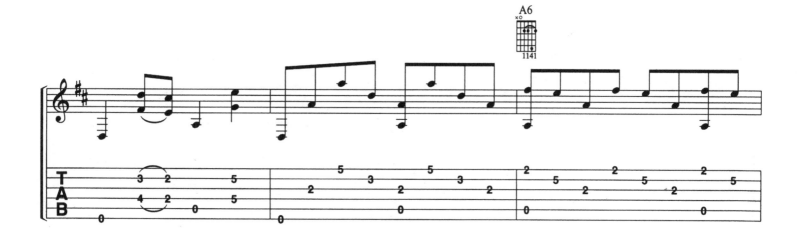

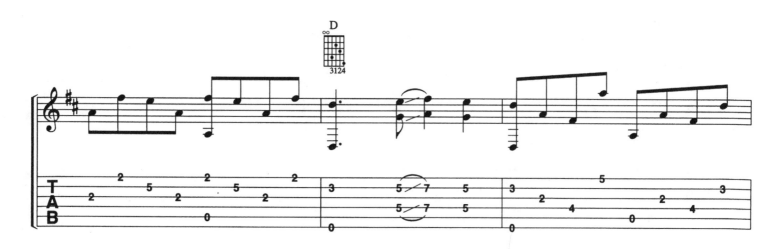

Never Going Back Again - 5 - 4

Never Going Back Again - 5 - 5

OLD MAN

Words and Music by
NEIL YOUNG

Old Man - 3 - 1

Chorus:

Old man, take a look at my life,— I'm a lot—— like— you.——

I—— need some-one to love— me the whole—— day—— through.—

Oh,—— one look in my eyes— and you can tell that's— true.——

1. w/Rhy. Fig. 2 *(Gtr. 1)*

2. w/Rhy. Fig. 1 *(Gtr. 1)*

D.S. % al Coda

Coda **Gtr. 1**

Old Man - 3 - 3

PANAMA

Words and Music by
EDWARD VAN HALEN, ALEX VAN HALEN
and DAVID LEE ROTH

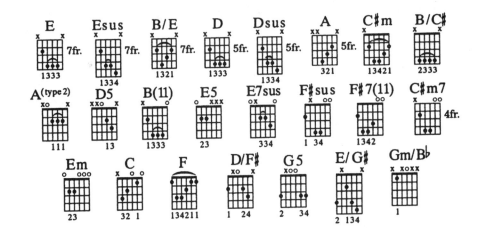

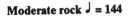

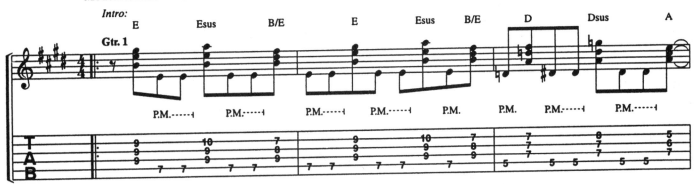

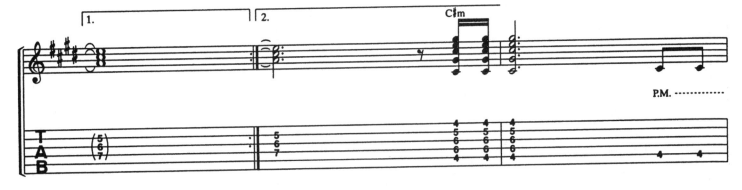

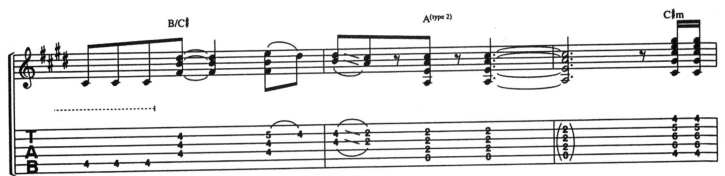

Panama - 7 - 1

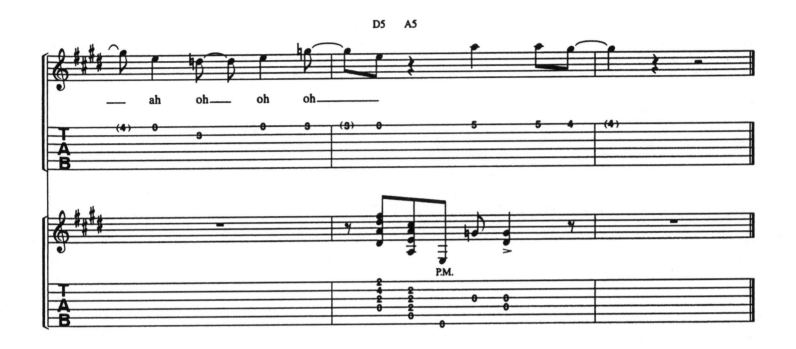

ah   oh___   oh   oh___

Verse 2:
Ain't nothin' like it, her shiny machine,
Got the feel for the wheel, keep the moving parts clean.
Hot shoe, burnin' down the avenue,
Got an on ramp comin' through my bedroom.
Don't you know she's comin' home to me?
You'll lose her in the turn.
I'll get her!
(To Chorus:)

PEACEFUL EASY FEELING

Words and Music by
JACK TEMPCHIN

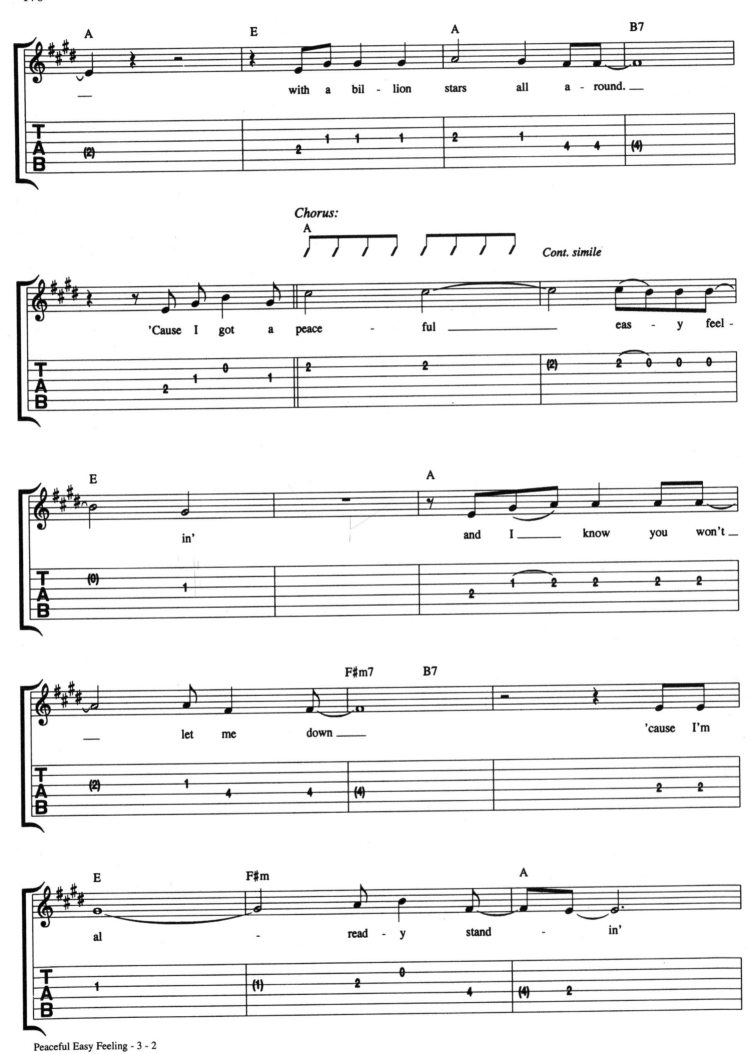

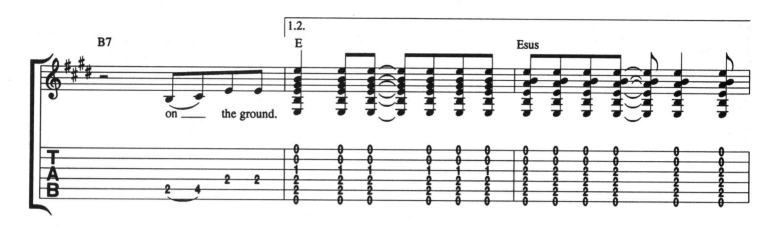

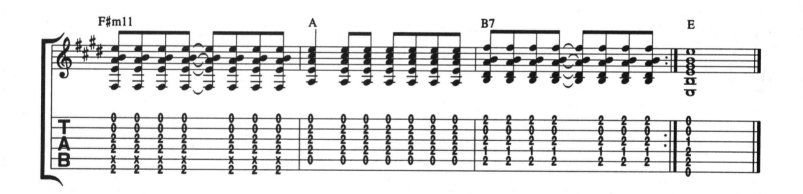

Verse 2:
And I found out a long time ago
What a woman can do to your soul.
Ah, but she can't take you anyway,
You don't already know how to go.
And I got a peaceful, easy feelin',
(To Chorus:)

Verse 3:
I get the feelin' I may know you
As a lover and a friend.
But this voice keeps whisperin' in my other ear,
Tells me I may never see you again.
'Cause I got a peaceful, easy feelin'.
(To Chorus:)

PROUD MARY

Words and Music by
JOHN C. FOGERTY

Proud Mary - 4 - 1

Proud Mary - 4 - 3

THE RIVER

Words and Music by
BRUCE SPRINGSTEEN

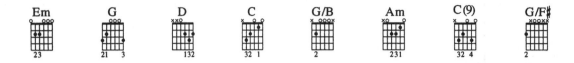

The River - 5 - 1

The River - 5 - 2

Verse 2:
Then I got Mary pregnant
And, man, that was all she wrote.
And for my nineteenth birthday,
I got a union card and a weddin' coat.
We went down to the courthouse
And the judge put it all to rest.
No weddin' day smiles,
No walk down the aisle,
No flowers, no weddin' dress.

Chorus 2:
That night, we went down to the river,
And into the river we'd drive.
Oh, down to the river we'd ride.
(To Verse 3:)

Verse 4:
But I remember us ridin' in my brother's car,
Her body tan and wet down at the reservoir.
At night on them banks, I'd lie awake
And pull her close just to feel each breath she'd take.
Now those memories come back to haunt me.
They haunt me like a curse.
Is a dream a lie if it don't come true?
Or is it somethin' worse that sends me…

Chorus 3:
Down to the river,
Though I know the river is dry.
That sends me down to the river tonight?

SANDMAN

Words and Music by
DEWEY BUNNELL

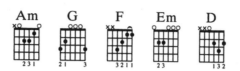

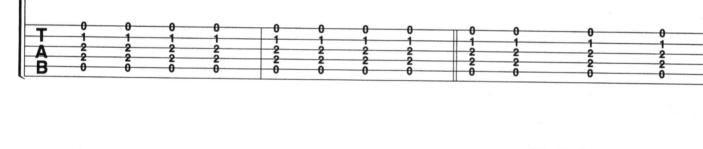

Sandman - 3 - 1

SHOWER THE PEOPLE

Words and Music by
JAMES TAYLOR

All gtrs. capo at 3rd fret to match recording

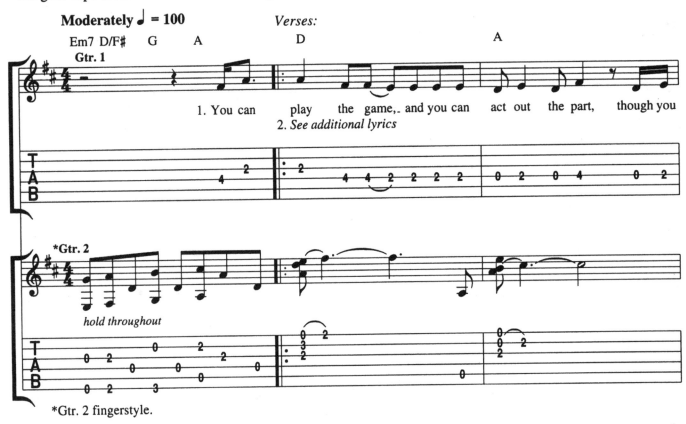

Shower the People - 5 - 1

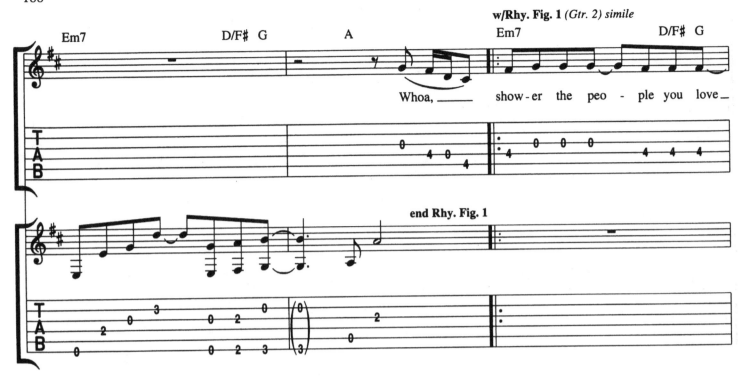

Verse 2:
Well, you can run but you cannot hide,
This is widely known.
And what you plan to do with your foolish pride
When you're all by yourself alone.
Once you tell somebody the way that you feel,
You can feel it beginning to ease.
I think it's true what they say,
About the squeaky wheel
Always getting the grease.

Chorus:
Better to shower the people you love with love;
Show them the way that you feel.
I know things are gonna be just fine if you only will.
What I'd like to do to you.
Shower the people you love with love;
Show them the way you feel.
Things are gonna be much better if you only will.

SUGAR MAGNOLIA

Words by
ROBERT HUNTER
Music by
BOB WEIR

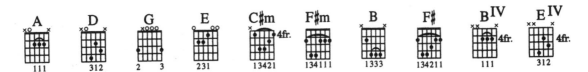

Moderately fast

Intro:

Verses:

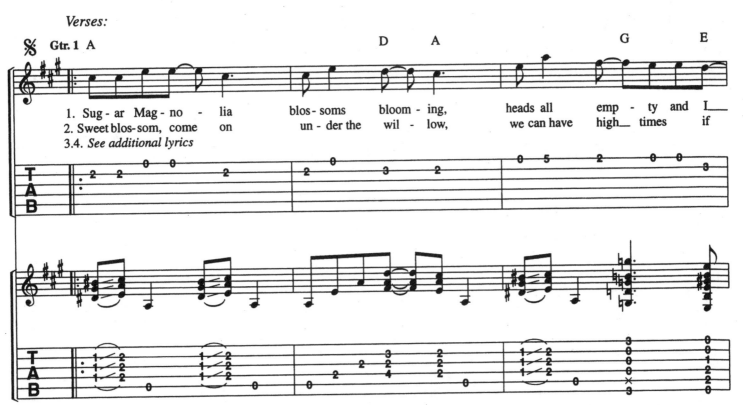

1. Sug - ar Mag - no - lia blos - soms bloom - ing, heads all emp - ty and I
2. Sweet blos - som, come on un - der the wil - low, we can have high times if
3.4. *See additional lyrics*

192

Coda

Sug-ar Mag-no - lia,   ring-ing the blue - bell,

(Gtr. 2 to rhy. slashes)

caught up in sun - light.   Come on out   sing-ing, I'll walk

— you in the sun - shine.   Oo,   come on hon - ey, come a - long with

me.

Sugar Magnolia - 7 - 4

Verse 3:
Well, she comes skimmin' through rays of violet,
She can wade in a drop of dew.
She don't come and I don't follow,
Waits backstage while I sing to you.

Verse 4:
Well, she can dance a Cajun rhythm,
Jump like a willys in four wheel drive.
She's a summer love in the spring, fall and winter.
She can make happy any man alive.
(To Chorus:)

SISTER GOLDEN HAIR

Words and Music by
GERRY BECKLEY

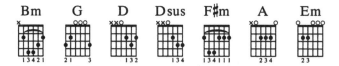

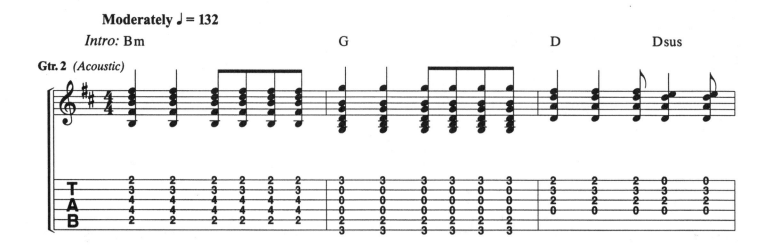

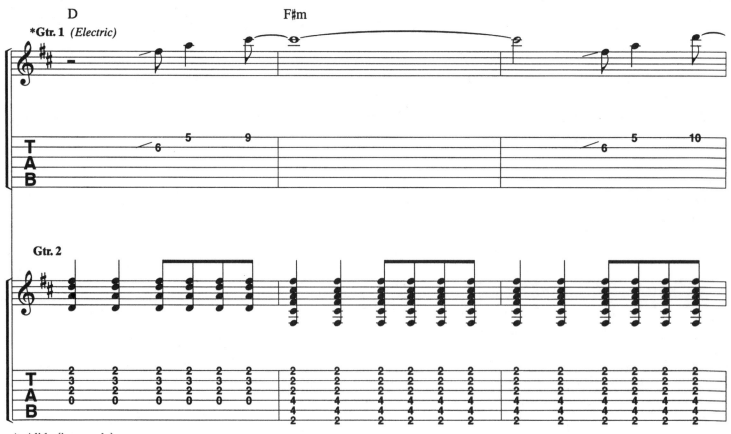

*w/slide (intro only).

Sister Golden Hair - 4 - 1

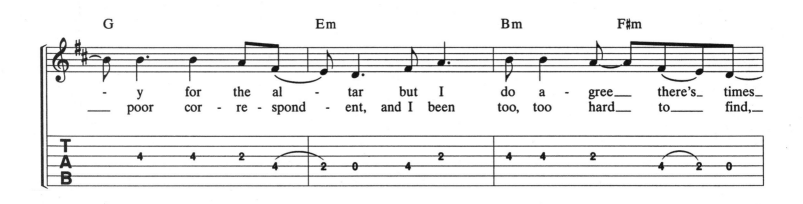

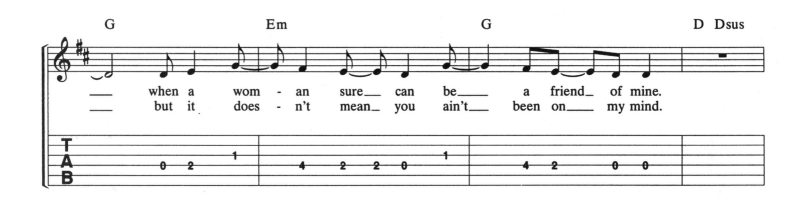

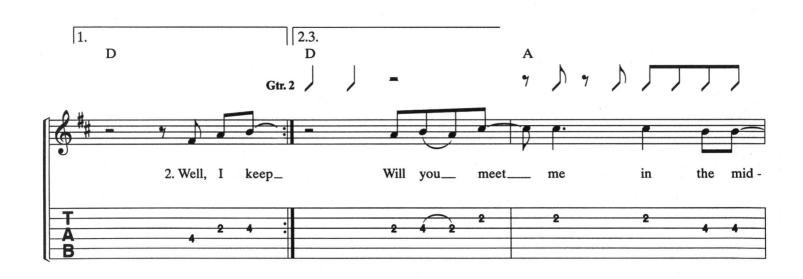

TAKE IT EASY

Words and Music by
JACKSON BROWNE and GLENN FREY

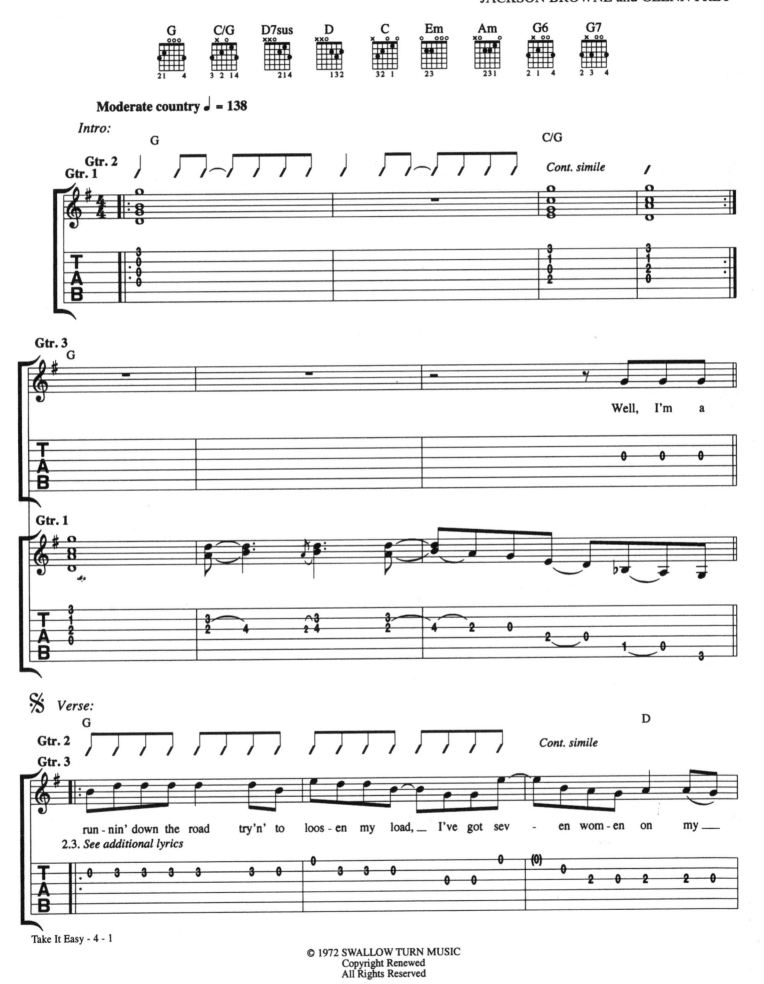

Take It Easy - 4 - 1

201

Take It Easy - 4 - 2

Verse 2:
Well, I'm a-standin' on a corner in Winslow, Arizona, and such a fine sight to see.
It's a girl, my Lord, in a flat-bed Ford slowin' down to take a look at me.
Come on, baby, don't say maybe,
I gotta know if your sweet love is gonna save me.
We may lose and we may win, though we will never be here again,
So open up, I'm climbin' in, so take it easy.

Verse 3:
Well, I'm a-runnin' down the road tryin' to loosen my load, got a world of trouble on my mind.
Lookin' for a lover who won't blow my cover, she's so hard to find.
Take it easy, take it easy.
Don't let the sound of your own wheels make you crazy
Come on baby, don't say maybe,
I gotta know if your sweet love is gonna save me.

TEQUILA SUNRISE

Words and Music by
DON HENLEY and GLENN FREY

Tequila Sunrise - 3 - 2

VENTURA HIGHWAY

Words and Music by
DEWEY BUNNELL

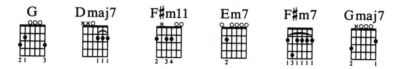

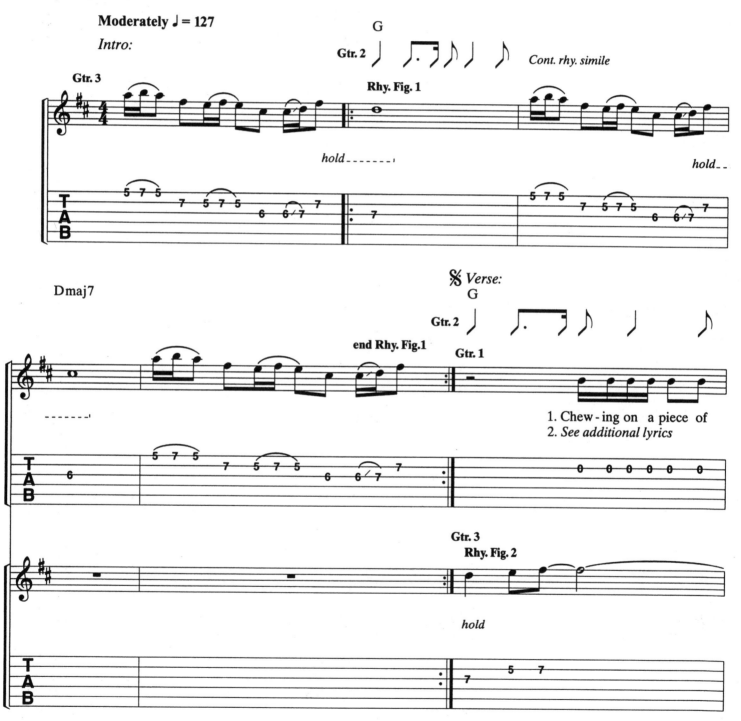

1. Chew-ing on a piece of
2. *See additional lyrics*

Ventura Highway - 5 - 1

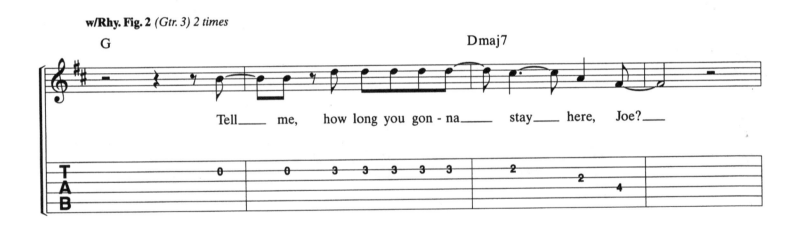

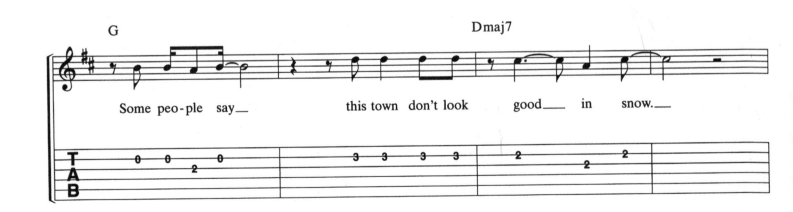

211

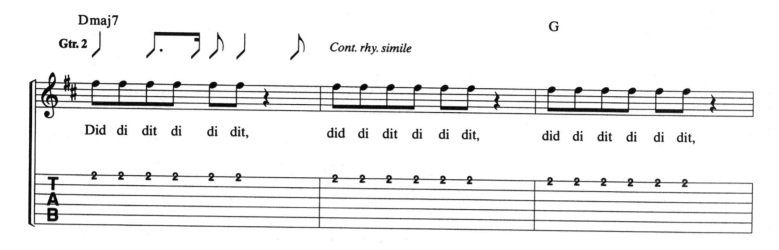

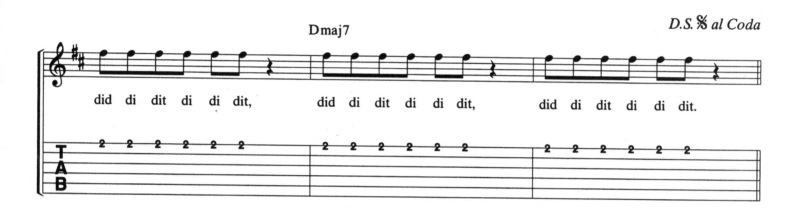

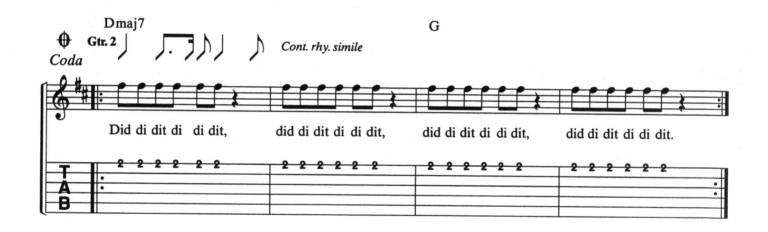

Verse 2:
Wishin' on a falling star,
Waitin' for the early train.
Sorry, boy, but I've been hit by purple rain.
Aw, come on, Joe,
You can always change your name.
Thanks a lot, son, just the same.
(To Chorus:)

TIN MAN

Words and Music by
DEWEY BUNNELL

Tin Man - 4 - 1

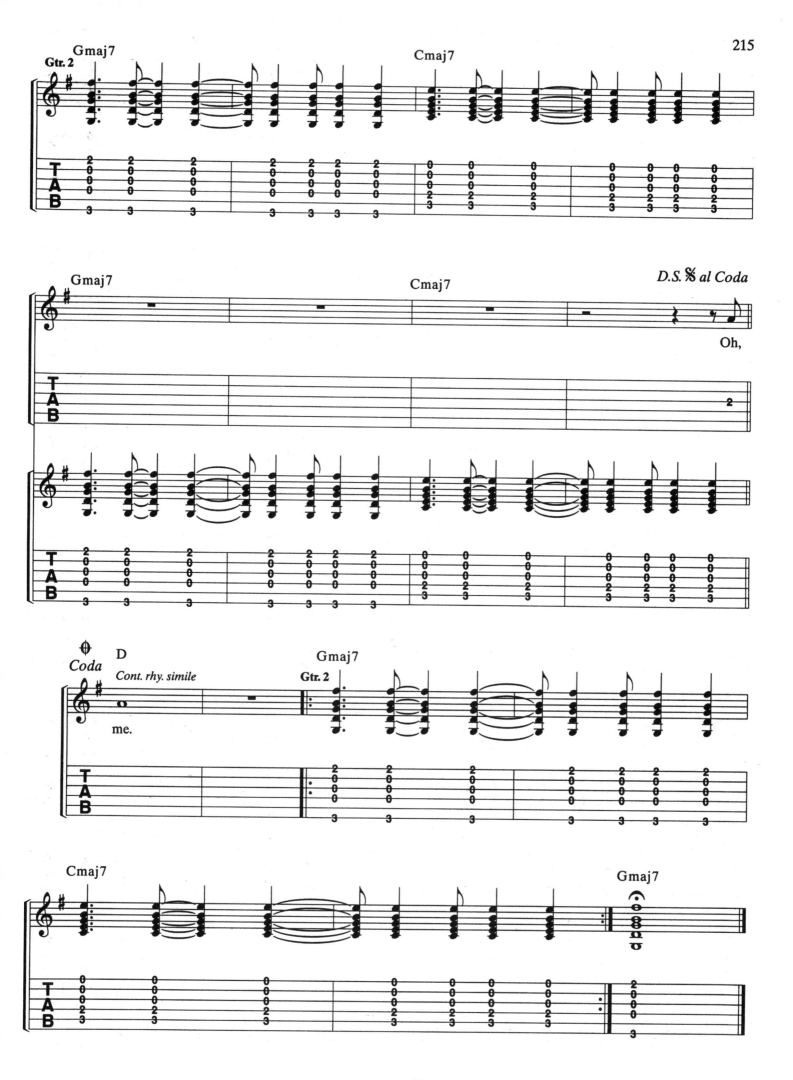

TRUCKIN'

Words by
ROBERT HUNTER
Music by
JERRY GARCIA, BOB WEIR
and PHIL LESH

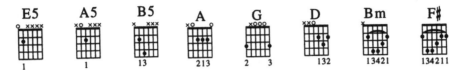

Truckin' - 8 - 1

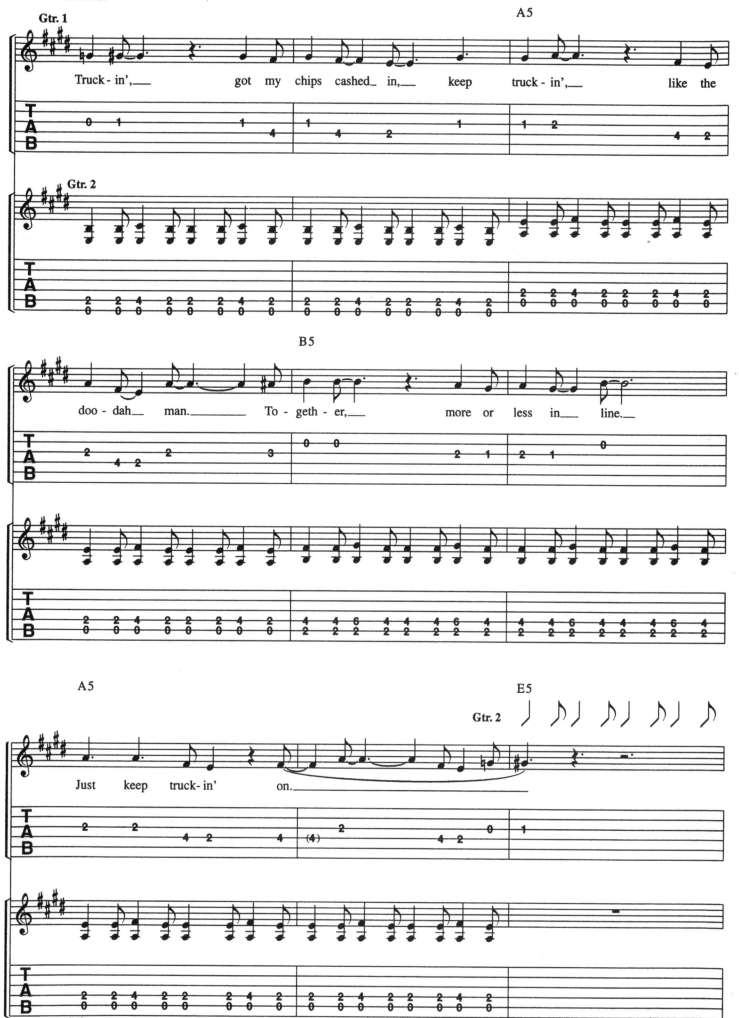

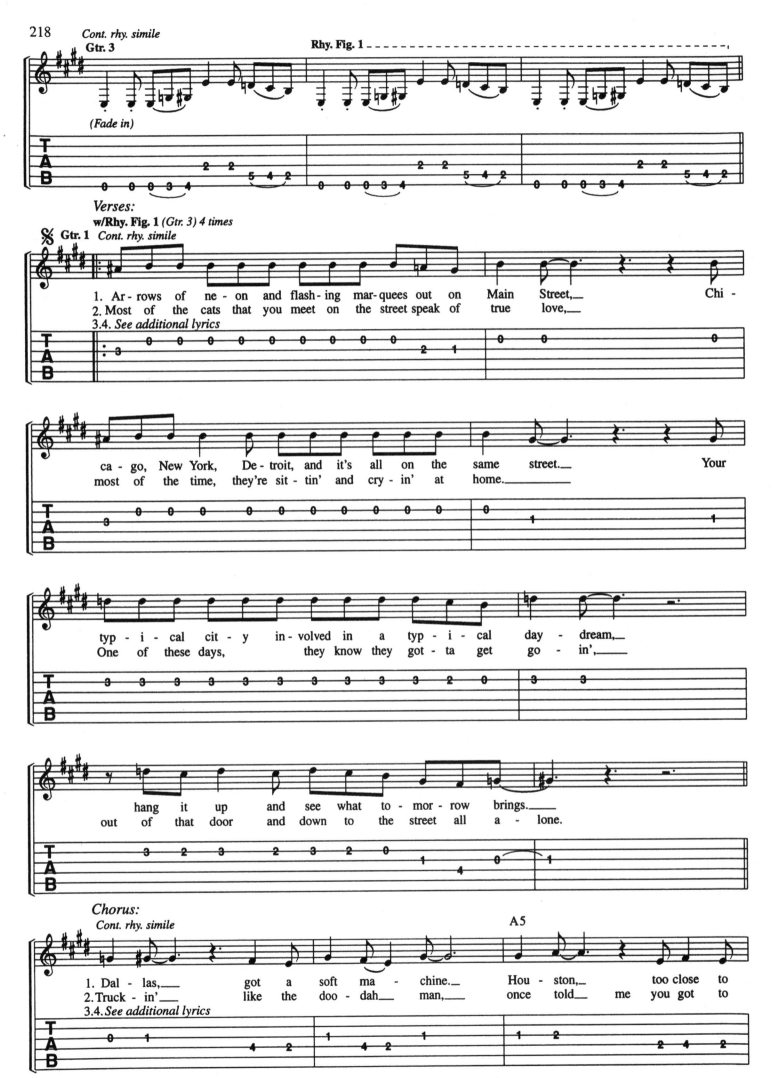

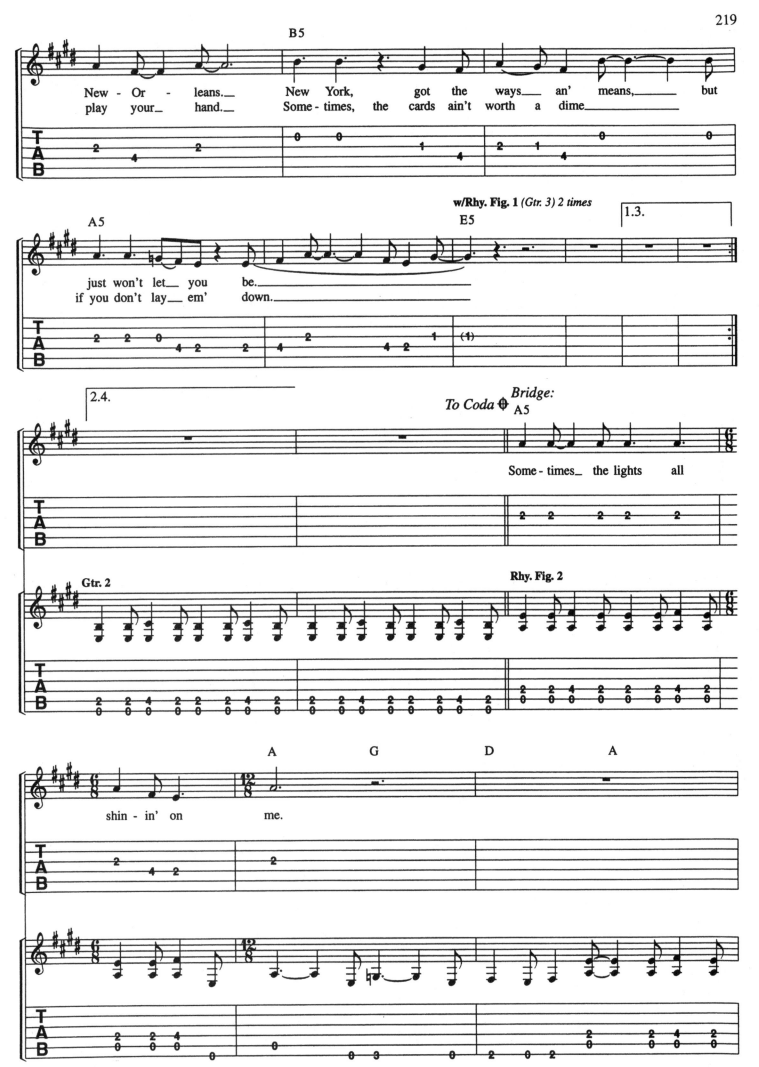

220

Truckin' - 8 - 5

Truckin' - 8 - 6

222

Truckin' - 8 - 7

Verse 3:
What in the world ever became of Sweet Jane?
She lost her sparkle, you know she isn't the same.
Livin' on reds, vitamin C and cocaine,
All a friend can say is ain't it a shame.
(To Chorus 3:)

Chorus 3:
Truckin',
Up to Buffalo,
Been thinkin',
You got to mellow slow.
Takes time
To pick a place to go,
And just keep truckin' on.
(To Verse 4:)

Verse 4:
Sittin' an' starin' out of the hotel window,
Got a tip they're gonna kick the door in again.
I'd like to get some sleep before I travel,
But if you got a warrant, I guess you're gonna come in.
(To Chorus 4:)

Chorus 4:
Busted,
Down on Bourbon street.
Set-up,
Like a bowlin' pin.
Knocked down,
It gets to wearing thin.
They just won't let you be.
(To Coda)

WHOLE LOTTA LOVE

Words and Music by
JIMMY PAGE, ROBERT PLANT,
JOHN PAUL JONES and JOHN BONHAM

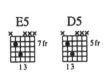

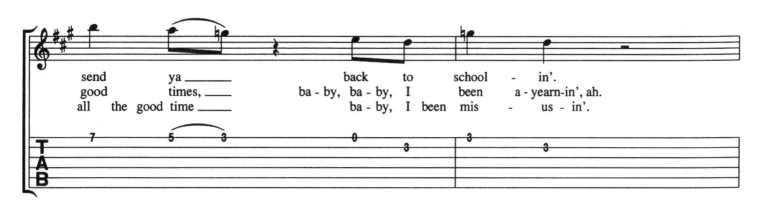

send   ya _____   back   to   school - in'.
good   times, _____   ba - by, ba - by,   I   been   a - yearn-in', ah.
all   the good time _____   ba - by, I   been   mis   -   us - in'.

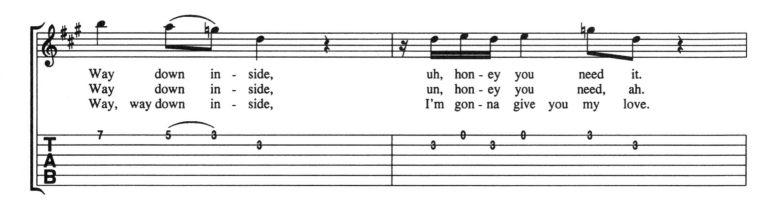

Way   down   in - side,   uh, hon - ey you   need   it.
Way   down   in - side,   un, hon - ey you   need,   ah.
Way, way down in - side,   I'm gon - na give you my   love.

I'm gon - na give you my   love, _____   I'm gon - na give you my   love. __ ⎫
I'm gon - na give you my   love, _____   I'm gon - na give you my   love. __ ⎬
I'm gon - na give you ev'ry inch of my love.   I'm gon - na give you my   love, __ ⎭

E5   D5   E5   D5

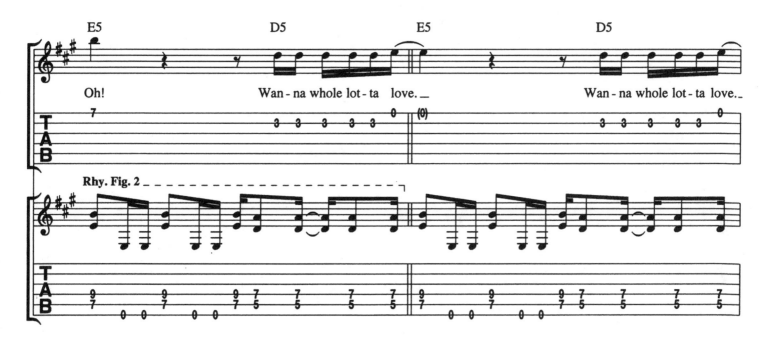

Oh!   Wan - na whole lot - ta love. __   Wan - na whole lot - ta love. __

Rhy. Fig. 2

Whole Lotta Love - 4 - 2

Whole Lotta Love - 4 - 4

THE WRECK OF
THE EDMUND FITZGERALD

All gtrs. capo 2nd fret to match recording.

Words and Music by
GORDON LIGHTFOOT

1. The

The Wreck of the Edmund Fitzgerald - 7 - 1

The Wreck of the Edmund Fitzgerald - 7 - 3

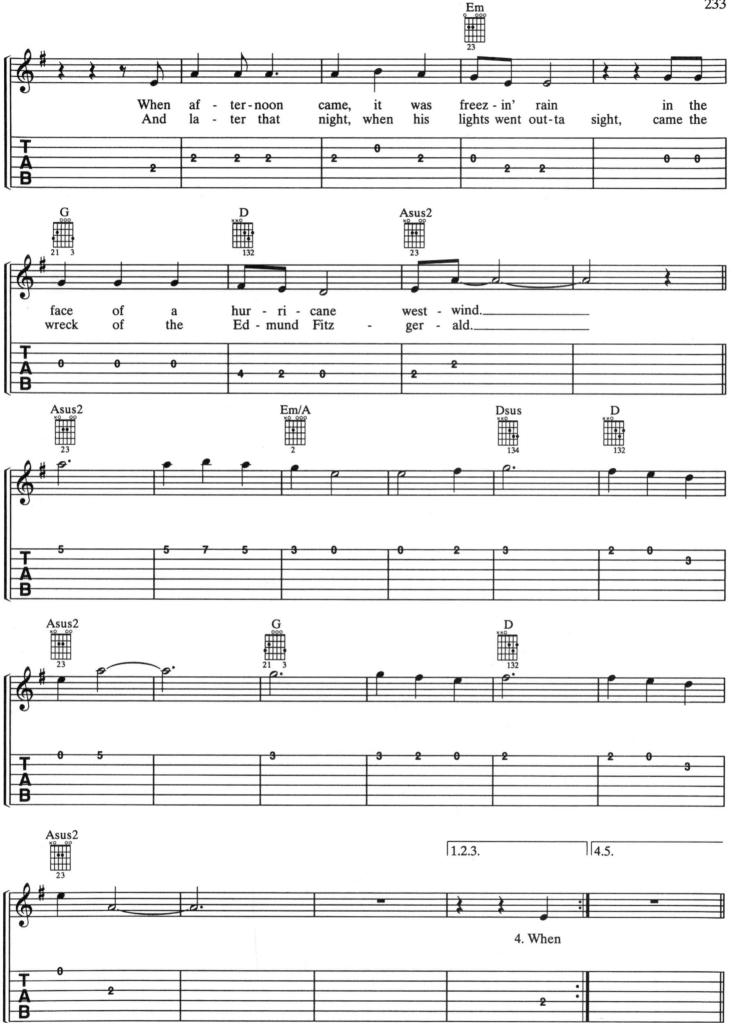

The Wreck of the Edmund Fitzgerald - 7 - 6

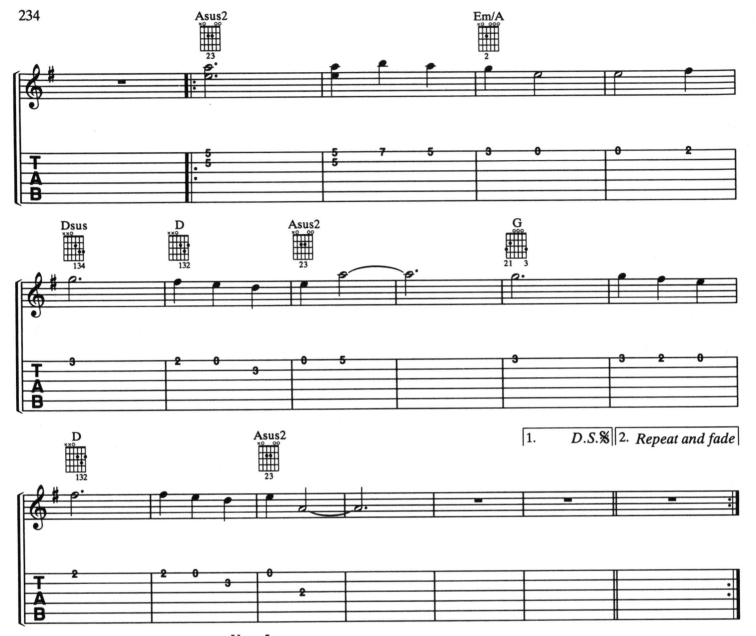

Verse 5:
Does any one know where the love of God goes
When the waves turn the minutes to hours?
The searches all say they'd have made Whitefish Bay
If they'd put fifteen more miles behind her.
They might have split up or they might have capsized;
May have broke deep and took water.
And all that remains is the faces and the names
Of the wives and the sons and the daughters.

Verse 6:
Lake Huron rolls, Superior sings
In the rooms of her ice-water mansion.
Old Michigan steams like a young man's dreams;
The islands and bays are for sportsmen.
And farther below Lake Ontario
Takes in what Lake Erie can send her,
And the iron boats go as the mariners all know
With the Gales of November remembered.

Verse 7:
In a musty old hall in Detroit they prayed,
In the "Maritime Sailors' Cathedral."
The church bell chimed till it rang twenty-nine times
For each man on the Edmund Fitzgerald.
The legend lives on from the Chippewa on down
Of the big lake they call "Gitche Gumee."
"Superior," they said, "never gives up her dead
When the 'Gales of November' come early!"

YOU REALLY GOT ME

Words and Music by
RAY DAVIES

You Really Got Me - 3 - 1

You Really Got Me - 3 - 3

GUITAR TAB GLOSSARY **

TABLATURE EXPLANATION

READING TABLATURE: Tablature illustrates the six strings of the guitar. Notes and chords are indicated by the placement of fret numbers on a given string(s).

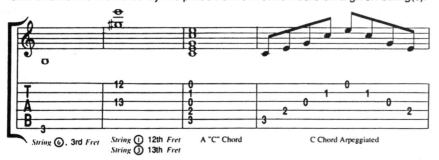

String ⑥, 3rd Fret   String ① 12th Fret   A "C" Chord   C Chord Arpeggiated
String ③ 13th Fret

BENDING NOTES

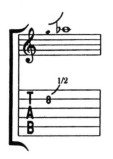

HALF STEP: Play the note and bend string one half step.*

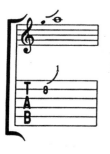

WHOLE STEP: Play the note and bend string one whole step.

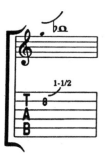

WHOLE STEP AND A HALF: Play the note and bend string a whole step and a half.

TWO STEPS: Play the note and bend string two whole steps.

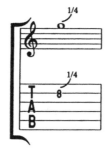

SLIGHT BEND (Microtone): Play the note and bend string slightly to the equivalent of half a fret.

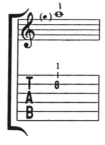

PREBEND (Ghost Bend): Bend to the specified note, before the string is picked.

PREBEND AND RELEASE: Bend the string, play it, then release to the original note.

REVERSE BEND: Play the already-bent string, then immediately drop it down to the fretted note.

BEND AND RELEASE: Play the note and gradually bend to the next pitch, then release to the original note. Only the first note is attacked.

BENDS INVOLVING MORE THAN ONE STRING: Play the note and bend string while playing an additional note (or notes) on another string(s). Upon release, relieve pressure from additional note(s), causing original note to sound alone.

BENDS INVOLVING STATIONARY NOTES: Play notes and bend lower pitch, then hold until release begins (indicated at the point where line becomes solid).

UNISON BEND: Play both notes and immediately bend the lower note to the same pitch as the higher note.

DOUBLE NOTE BEND: Play both notes and immediately bend both strings simultaneously.

*A half step is the smallest interval in Western music; it is equal to one fret. A whole step equals two frets.

© 1990 Beam Me Up Music
c/o CPP/Belwin, Inc. Miami, Florida 33014
International Copyright Secured   Made in U.S.A.   All Rights Reserved   **By Kenn Chipkin and Aaron Stang

RHYTHM SLASHES

STRUM INDICATIONS: Strum with indicated rhythm.

The chord voicings are found on the first page of the transcription underneath the song title.

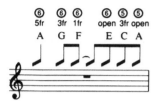

INDICATING SINGLE NOTES USING RHYTHM SLASHES: Very often single notes are incorporated into a rhythm part. The note name is indicated above the rhythm slash with a fret number and a string indication.

ARTICULATIONS

HAMMER ON: Play lower note, then "hammer on" to higher note with another finger. Only the first note is attacked.

LEFT HAND HAMMER: Hammer on the first note played on each string with the left hand.

PULL OFF: Play higher note, then "pull off" to lower note with another finger. Only the first note is attacked.

FRET-BOARD TAPPING: "Tap" onto the note indicated by + with a finger of the pick hand, then pull off to the following note held by the fret hand.

TAP SLIDE: Same as fretboard tapping, but the tapped note is slid randomly up the fretboard, then pulled off to the following note.

BEND AND TAP TECHNIQUE: Play note and bend to specified interval. While holding bend, tap onto note indicated.

LEGATO SLIDE: Play note and slide to the following note. (Only first note is attacked).

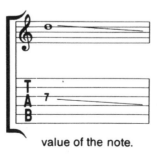

LONG GLISSANDO: Play note and slide in specified direction for the full value of the note.

SHORT GLISSANDO: Play note for its full value and slide in specified direction at the last possible moment.

PICK SLIDE: Slide the edge of the pick in specified direction across the length of the string(s).

MUTED STRINGS: A percussive sound is made by laying the fret hand across all six strings while pick hand strikes specified area (low, mid, high strings).

PALM MUTE: The note or notes are muted by the palm of the pick hand by lightly touching the string(s) near the bridge.

TREMOLO PICKING: The note or notes are picked as fast as possible.

TRILL: Hammer on and pull off consecutively and as fast as possible between the original note and the grace note.

ACCENT: Notes or chords are to be played with added emphasis.

STACCATO (Detached Notes): Notes or chords are to be played roughly half their actual value and with separation.

DOWN STROKES AND UPSTROKES: Notes or chords are to be played with either a downstroke (⊓ ·) or upstroke (∨) of the pick.

VIBRATO: The pitch of a note is varied by a rapid shaking of the fret hand finger, wrist, and forearm.

HARMONICS

NATURAL HARMONIC: A finger of the fret hand lightly touches the note or notes indicated in the tab and is played by the pick hand.

ARTIFICIAL HARMONIC: The first tab number is fretted, then the pick hand produces the harmonic by using a finger to lightly touch the same string at the second tab number (in parenthesis) and is then picked by another finger.

ARTIFICIAL "PINCH" HAR-MONIC: A note is fretted as indicated by the tab, then the pick hand produces the harmonic by squeezing the pick firmly while using the tip of the index finger in the pick attack. If parenthesis are found around the fretted note, it does not sound. No parenthesis means both the fretted note and A.H. are heard simultaneously.

TREMOLO BAR

SPECIFIED INTERVAL: The pitch of a note or chord is lowered to a specified interval and then may or may not return to the original pitch. The activity of the tremolo bar is graphically represented by peaks and valleys.

UN-SPECIFIED INTERVAL: The pitch of a note or a chord is lowered to an unspecified interval.